FEASTING ON
FISH

FEASTING ON
FISH

LOUISE PICKFORD

Photographs by Gus Filgate

SMITHMARK

Copyright © 1995 Salamander Books Limited London

1   3   5   7   9   8   6   4   2

ISBN 0-8317-3166-4

This edition published in 1995 by SMITHMARK Publishers Inc.
16 East 32nd Street. New York, NY 10016

SMITHMARK books are available for bulk purchase for sales promotion
and premium use. For details write to or call the manager of special sales,
SMITHMARK Publishers Inc., 16 East 32nd Street, New York, NY 10016;
(212) 532-6600

CREDITS
Managing Editor: ANNE MCDOWALL
Copy Editor: VERONICA SPERLING
Designer: PETER BRIDGEWATER
Photographer: GUS FILGATE
Home Economist: MAXINE CLARK
Stylist: JANE MCLEISH
Typesetting: CHRIS LANAWAY
Indexer: ALISON LEACH
Color reproduction:
P & W GRAPHICS PTE. LTD., SINGAPORE
Printed in Italy

CONTENTS

INTRODUCTION

≈

A great many varieties of exotic fish are appearing in our stores and fish vendors allowing us to become more adventurous with what we cook. Eating fish has great nutritional benefits too – it is a good source of protein (particularly oily fish and shellfish) and many types are low in saturated fats. Cooking times are short for many fish dishes, making fish an ideal choice for today's busy cook.

Whenever possible, shop for, cook and eat fish on the same day. If you really need to shop in advance, scale, gut, wash and dry the fish and wrap it loosely in foil. Store it in the refrigerator overnight, but no longer. When buying fish, ensure that the gills are bright red and moist. The eyes should also be bright and moist; avoid cloudy shrunken eyes. The flesh should be firm without being over springy and a clean fresh smell of the sea should be the only odor. When buying live shellfish, choose those that look the liveliest. Clams and mussel shells should be tightly closed.

Preparing fish and shellfish

Scaling, gutting and filleting fish is actually very easy, but most fish vendors will be happy to do this for you if you wish; I always ask mine to scale the fish, and I would advise you to ask your fish vendor to gut the fish for you as well. Make sure you are armed with a very sharp filleting knife.

To fillet round fish, such as salmon, trout and mackerel, remove the head and tail and cut along one side of the backbone from head to tail. Keeping the knife at a slight angle, close to the backbone, work the top fillet away from the bones with a sawing motion. Turn the fish over and repeat with the second fillet.

To fillet flat fish, such as flounder and sole, place the fish onto a board with the head away from you and cut down one side of the backbone. Insert the knife between flesh and bone and cut the fillet away with a slight sawing motion. Repeat with the second fillet. Turn the fish over and repeat as above.

To skin a whole flat fish, start with the dark skin and cut across the skin below the head and above the tail. Hold the tail firmly with paper towel and pull the skin from the head away in one whole piece. Turn the fish over and repeat with the white skin, if wished.

To skin fish fillets, place the fillet skin side down on a board and insert a sharp knife between flesh and skin. Work the knife along the length of the fillet with a slight sawing motion to free the flesh from the skin.

To prepare mussels and clams, discard any open shells and rinse the mussels or clams in running cold water for several minutes. Place them in a large bowl, cover with cold water and sprinkle over some brown flour or oatmeal. Leave to soak in a cool place for several hours. Wash again under running water and scrub the shells. Pull away the beard that often hangs down from the closed shell. Rinse again in several changes of cold water before cooking.

To clean squid, pull the head and tentacles away from the body, bringing the gut out of the body cavity. Reserve the tentacles, but discard the head and sharp 'beak'. Skin the squid by pulling it away from the body. Discard the 'wings' if wished. Wash the body cavity inside and out.

To shell and de-vein shrimps, cut off the head and pull away the legs. Ease away and peel off the shell from the underneath of the shrimp. Reserve the heads and shells; they make good stock. Using a sharp knife cut along the center of the back and pull out and discard the black intestinal vein.

Cooking fish and shellfish

Poaching, stewing and steaming tend to keep a fish more moist than baking, broiling or barbecuing.

STEWING Fish can be stewed either whole or in pieces, cooked in flavored stocks or sauces, where both fish and liquid are eaten as part of the dish. Stews are often made using a selection of vegetables, herbs, spices and stock.

STEAMING Whole fish, fillets or steaks are steamed in either a double boiler, or a fish kettle, over stock, where the delicate flavors can be enjoyed at their best. Often fish is cooked over a highly flavored broth of marinade to impart flavor.

BROILING Fish can be broiled under an oven broiler, or over charcoal, which adds an intense flavor to the dish. Baste the fish with oil, butter or marinade as it cooks to prevent it becoming dry.

BAKING Fish can be open roasted in the oven, or cooked in a covered casserole or in a paper envelope (en papillote). Once in the oven you can forget about it until ready to serve, making this an ideal cooking method for a dinner party.

PAN FRYING This method is most commonly used to cook fillets, steaks or pieces of fish. Use a heavy non-stick skillet and shallow fry the fish in oil or butter.

DEEP FRYING Use a deep, heavy-based pan, good-quality cooking oil and a sugar thermometer to successfully deep fry fish, which can be coated either in batter or in a little flour. The oil should reach approximately 360°F before you add the fish.

POACHING Cooking fish in a barely simmering liquid keeps it moist and tender. The liquid varies, but is generally plain water or court bouillon. Fish stock is often used if the stock is to be used as the basis of a sauce. Milk is usually used to poach smoked fish, as it helps to draw out excess saltiness. Beer and cider can also be used for poaching.

COURT BOUILLON

≈

2½ cups water	1 garlic clove
2½ cups dry white wine	2 bay leaves
3 tbsp white wine vinegar	2 sprigs fresh parsley
2 carrots, sliced	2 sprigs fresh thyme
1 onion, chopped	6 white peppercorns
1 leek, sliced	1 tsp salt
2 celery stalks, sliced	

≈

Place all the ingredients in a saucepan, bring slowly to a boil, cover and simmer for 30 minutes. Strain, and return to the pan. Boil rapidly for about 10 minutes until reduced to 2½ cups. Refrigerate until required.

FISH STOCK

≈

Prepare as for Court Bouillon, increasing the water and wine to 1 quart, and adding 2 pounds fish heads and trimmings. Boil until reduced to 1 quart.

SOUPS AND STEWS

FISH AND SEAFOOD combined with a stock provide a delicious range of satisfying soups, broths and stews. The basis for many of these recipes, especially for those dishes that have a delicate flavor, is a good quality fish stock (see page 7). Other dishes that contain more robust ingredients, imparting a richer and more intense flavor, can be made with vegetable stock. Make fish stock in large quantities and freeze some for future use. Ask your fishvendor to set aside some fish heads and bones to make the stock, these are usually available free of charge. I have included soups and stews from around the world, many of which are my versions of classic recipes. These range from quick and easy family dishes, such as Italian Fish Broth with Broccoli and Pasta, to more elaborate stews, which are ideal for entertaining, such as Exotic Seafood Stew and Tuna Fish Stew with Couscous.

CONTENTS

≋

EXOTIC SEAFOOD STEW

Serves 4

Based on a classic Spanish dish, this rich medley
of seafood is a visual feast. Although the
cooking time is quick, it is important to have all
the ingredients ready before you begin cooking,
to insure success.

~~~

*2 small cooked lobsters
(1 pound each)
4 tbsp olive oil
2 onions, chopped
2 garlic cloves, chopped
4 beef tomatoes, peeled
and chopped
¼ tsp powdered saffron
or turmeric
2 tbsp chopped fresh parsley
1 dried red chili, seeded
and chopped
1 pound monkfish
fillet, cubed
Seasoned flour
6 fresh crawfish
6 raw jumbo shrimp*

*4 small squid (about 1¼
pounds), cleaned (see pages
6-7) and cut into rings
18 fresh mussels, scrubbed
18 fresh small clams, washed
4 tbsp brandy
⅓ cup dry white wine
⅔ cup Fish Stock (see page 7)
1 tsp salt*
S A U C E
*2 slices stale white bread,
crumbled
1 tbsp red wine vinegar
1 tbsp olive oil
¼ cup cashew nuts, toasted
Pepper
Chopped fresh parsley,
to garnish*

Prepare the lobsters: separate the head and body, and
break off the 2 claws from each lobster. Set aside.

Heat 1 tablespoon of the oil in a skillet, and fry the
onion and garlic for 5 minutes. Add the tomatoes, saffron,
parsley and chili, and fry for a further 10 minutes.
Transfer to a large flameproof casserole.

Dust the monkfish in a little seasoned flour. Heat the
remaining oil in the skillet, add the monkfish, crawfish,
shrimp and squid, in that order, and fry until browned.
Add to the casserole with the mussels, clams and prepared
lobster.

Pour the brandy into the skillet, ignite and flame.
When the flames die down, pour any juices into the
casserole with the wine, stock and salt. Bring to a boil,
then cover and simmer for 10 minutes.

Meanwhile, prepare the sauce. Soak the bread in the
vinegar and oil for 10 minutes. Add the nuts, and 6 tablespoons of the cooking juices from the casserole, and purée
in a blender until smooth. Stir back into the casserole
until combined, and simmer for a further 3-4 minutes,
until the sauce is thickened.

Adjust the seasoning, garnish with the chopped parsley,
and serve at once straight from the dish, with plenty of
bread to mop up the juices.

TUNISIAN MUSSEL SOUP

Serves 4

A rich Tunisian soup of both puréed and whole mussels is topped with a tangy lemon and chili garnish.

2 pounds fresh small mussels, scrubbed	14-ounce can plum tomatoes, mashed
Pinch of saffron strands	2 tbsp chopped fresh cilantro
1 tbsp olive oil	Salt and pepper
1 onion, chopped	**GARNISH**
2 garlic cloves, chopped	4 tbsp olive oil
Grated zest and juice of	1 shallot, thinly sliced
1 lemon	Grated zest and juice of
1 tsp paprika	½ lemon
1 tsp ground cumin	½ small dried red chili, seeded
Pinch of cayenne pepper	and sliced
	1 tsp fresh thyme leaves

Place the mussels in a large pan with just the water left on the shells after scrubbing. Steam for 5-6 minutes until the shells have opened. Discard any that remain closed.

Strain the cooking liquid into a bowl and make up to 2½ cups with water. Add the saffron strands and leave to soak. Remove the mussels from their shells.

Heat the oil in a large pan, and fry the onion, garlic, lemon zest and spices for 5 minutes. Add the tomatoes, reserved saffron stock, half the cooked mussels, and the lemon juice. Bring to a boil, cover and simmer for 20 minutes.

Purée the soup in a blender until very smooth, then return to the pan. Add the remaining mussels, the cilantro and seasoning, heat through, and keep warm.

For the garnish, heat the oil, and fry the shallot for 5 minutes until golden. Add the lemon zest and chili, fry for 3 minutes, stir in the lemon juice and thyme, and remove from the heat. Serve the soup in individual bowls, and spoon over the garnish.

NORTH AFRICAN FISH STEW

Serves 6

This is an unusual tasting, but quite delicious stew using a selection of fish and fish fillets. The addition of dates and peanuts gives an authentic North African flavor.

1 large eggplant, chopped	1 large mackerel, cleaned and
4 tbsp groundnut oil	cut into 1-inch steaks
6 ounces button mushrooms	1 small grey mullet, scaled,
1 large onion, chopped	cleaned and cut into steaks
1 garlic clove, chopped	8 ounces firm white fish fillets
2 green chilies, seeded	Juice of 3 limes
and chopped	⅔ cup vegetable stock
1 tsp paprika	⅔ cup fresh dates, stoned and
1 tsp ground cumin	chopped
1 pound ripe tomatoes,	½ cup peanuts, toasted and
chopped	roughly ground
	Salt and pepper

Preheat the oven to 400°F. Place the eggplant in a roasting pan and toss with half the oil. Bake on the top shelf of the oven for 20 minutes until browned and tender.

Heat the remaining oil in a large pan, and stir-fry the mushrooms for 3 minutes. Remove with a slotted spoon, and set aside. Add the onion, garlic, chili and spices to the pan, and fry for 5 minutes. Add the eggplant, mushrooms, tomatoes, fish, lime juice and stock. Bring to a boil, cover and simmer for 20 minutes.

Add the dates and peanuts to the stew, and simmer for a further 5 minutes until the fish is cooked through.

Season to taste, and serve at once with boiled rice or plenty of bread to soak up the juices.

Top: NORTH AFRICAN FISH STEW
Bottom: TUNISIAN MUSSEL SOUP

SICILIAN SALT COD

Serves 4 - 6

Dried, salted cod must be soaked in plenty of cold water in order to soften the flesh and remove excess saltiness. I first tasted salt cod in Sicily cooked in a similar way to this recipe.

2 pounds salt cod	½ cup pitted black olives, halved
Milk	
4 tbsp seasoned flour	2 tbsp balsamic vinegar
4 tbsp olive oil	⅔ cup chicken or vegetable stock
8 ounces baby onions, halved	
2 garlic cloves, chopped	2 tbsp tomato paste
4 ripe tomatoes, chopped	1 tsp sugar
⅔ cup golden raisins	Pepper
	2 tbsp chopped fresh parsley

Wash the salt cod, place in a bowl, and cover with cold water. Leave to soak for 12 hours, changing the water several times, if possible.

Drain the fish, rinse under cold running water, and pat dry. Remove the skin, and cube the flesh. Place in a shallow dish, cover with milk, and leave to soak for a further 2 hours. Wash the fish again, pat dry, and dust lightly in the seasoned flour.

Heat half the oil in a non-stick skillet, add the cod, and cook for 3 minutes until browned. Remove with a slotted spoon, and set aside.

Add the remaining oil to the skillet, and fry the onions and garlic for 5 minutes until golden. Add the remaining ingredients except the parsley, bring to a boil, cover and simmer for 20 minutes.

Return the cod to the skillet, sprinkle over the parsley, and simmer for a further 10-15 minutes until the fish is cooked. Season, and serve with rice, pasta or bread.

TUNA FISH STEW WITH COUSCOUS

Serves 4 - 6

Couscous is usually served with a meat or vegetable stew, but here tuna, a very meaty fish, is used to make a tasty alternative.

3 cups couscous	1 pound mixed vegetables (e.g. carrots, fennel, celery, parsnip), sliced
2½ cups cold water	
1½ pounds fresh tuna steak	
4 tbsp olive oil	2 cups tomato juice
1 red onion, cut into wedges	1 cup vegetable stock
2 garlic cloves, chopped	175 g/6 oz cooked chickpeas
2 tsp ground coriander	½ cup golden raisins
1 tsp ground cumin	2 tbsp chopped fresh cilantro
1 tsp ground cinnamon	¼ cup pine nuts, toasted
¼ tsp cayenne pepper	Fresh cilantro sprigs, to garnish

Place the couscous in a bowl, pour over the water, and set aside for 30 minutes for the grains to soften.

Cut the tuna into 1-inch cubes. Heat half the oil in a large pan, and quickly brown the tuna on all sides. Remove with a slotted spoon, and set aside.

Add the remaining oil to the pan, and fry the onion, garlic and spices for 5 minutes, then add the vegetables, and fry for a further 5 minutes. Stir in the tomato juice and stock, bring to a boil, cover and simmer for 20 minutes. Add the tuna, chickpeas, golden raisins and cilantro to the pan, and cook for a further 15 minutes.

Meanwhile, cook the couscous according to the instructions on the package. Spoon the couscous onto a large platter. Using a slotted spoon, arrange the fish and vegetables over the couscous. Sprinkle over the nuts, garnish with cilantro, and serve the juices separately.

Top: TUNA FISH STEW WITH COUSCOUS
Bottom: SICILIAN SALT COD

STEWED SQUID WITH GARLIC CROSTINI

Serves 4

Based on a favorite dish I frequently enjoy at a local Italian restaurant, this squid stew makes a wonderful starter.

2 pounds squid, cleaned (see pages 6-7)	*2 tbsp tomato paste*
2 tbsp olive oil	*½ cup pitted black olives, halved*
1 onion, sliced	*4 thick slices day-old bread*
3 celery stalks, sliced	*2 garlic cloves, halved*
1 garlic clove, crushed	*salt and pepper*
1 tbsp chopped fresh thyme	**GARNISH**
⅔ cup red wine	*Lemon wedges*
2 tbsp red wine vinegar	*Flat-leafed parsley*
3 beef tomatoes, peeled, seeded and chopped	

Cut the squid into ½-inch thick slices. Heat the oil in a pan, and quickly fry the squid until browned. Add the onion, celery, garlic and thyme, and fry for 10 minutes.

Add the wine, boil rapidly for 3 minutes, then add the vinegar, tomatoes and tomato paste. Cover and simmer for 45 minutes, until the squid is really tender. Stir in the olives.

Preheat the oven to 400°F. Prepare the crostini: place the sliced bread on a baking sheet, and bake for 15 minutes until crisp, turning once. Allow to cool slightly, and rub all over with the garlic halves.

Place a slice of bread in each serving bowl, spoon over the squid and broth, and serve immediately, garnished with lemon wedges and flat-leafed parsley.

FISH BROTH WITH BROCCOLI AND PASTA

Serves 4

This Italian soup is more of a stew than a soup and is a meal in itself. Serve with Italian-style bread and pass around some freshly grated Parmesan cheese.

½ small onion, very finely chopped	*¼ tsp freshly ground black pepper*
1 garlic clove, crushed	*1 tbsp olive oil*
¼ cup sun-dried tomatoes in oil, drained and chopped	*1 quart Fish Stock (see pages 6-7)*
4 anchovy fillets canned in oil, drained and chopped	*6 ounces broccoli florets*
1 tbsp chopped fresh parsley	*¾ cup conchiglie pasta shapes*
	Freshly grated Parmesan cheese, to serve

Place the onion, garlic, tomatoes, anchovies, parsley, and pepper in a blender, and purée to form a fairly smooth paste.

Heat the oil in a large pan, add the paste, and fry gently for 5 minutes. Add the stock and bring to a boil. Stir in the broccoli and pasta, return to a boil, and simmer for 8-10 minutes, until the broccoli is cooked and the pasta is al dente.

Season to taste, and serve hot with freshly grated Parmesan and bread.

Top: FISH BROTH WITH BROCCOLI AND PASTA
Bottom: STEWED SQUID WITH GARLIC CROSTINI

SOUPE AUX POISSONS

Serves 4

This is my version of the classic French dish, a creamy puréed soup full of the intense flavors of the sea.

≈≈≈

8 ounces cooked shrimp in shells	1 quart vegetable stock
2 tbsp butter	1 tbsp Worcestershire sauce or few drops of Tabasco sauce
1 onion, chopped	½ cup walnuts, toasted and ground
2 garlic cloves, chopped	2 tbsp tomato paste
2 ripe tomatoes, chopped	**TO SERVE**
2 sprigs fresh parsley	½ quantity Garlic Sauce (see page 32), optional
2 sprigs fresh thyme	Croûtons
8 ounces cod or haddock steaks	Freshly grated Parmesan cheese
⅔ cup dry cider or dry white wine	

≈≈≈

Peel the shrimp, and reserve the heads, shells and flesh.

Melt the butter in a large pan, and fry the onion and garlic for 3 minutes. Add the shrimp shells and heads, tomatoes, herbs and fish, and fry for a further 3 minutes.

Pour in the cider or wine, boil rapidly for 3 minutes, then add the stock and Worcestershire sauce or Tabasco. Cover and simmer for 30 minutes.

Purée the soup in a blender until smooth, and pass through a fine strainer into a clean pan.

Place the shrimp in a blender with the walnuts, tomato paste and 2 tbsp of the puréed fish soup, and blend to form a thick paste. Whisk the paste back into the soup, and simmer for 5 minutes until thickened.

Spoon the soup into warmed serving bowls, stir in a spoonful of the garlic sauce (if using), and top with croûtons and Parmesan.

FISH STEWED IN RED WINE

Serves 4

The addition of red wine gives a wonderful depth of flavor to this delicious stew. Discard the heads and tails of the fish if wished.

≈≈≈

4 small red snapper or silver bream (about 8 ounces each), scaled and cleaned	1 tbsp fennel seeds
2 tbsp all-purpose flour	1 pound ripe tomatoes, chopped (or 14-ounce can chopped tomatoes)
4 tbsp olive oil	2½ cups red wine
8 ounces button mushrooms	2 bay leaves
1 onion, sliced	4 sprigs fresh thyme
1 garlic clove, chopped	Salt and pepper
1 red bell pepper, seeded and chopped	Chopped fresh thyme, to garnish
2 potatoes, diced	

≈≈≈

Wash and dry the fish, and dust lightly with the flour.

Heat the oil in a large wide pan, and fry the fish on both sides for 2-3 minutes until golden. Remove with a slotted spoon and set aside. Add the mushrooms to the pan, and fry for 3 minutes until golden. Remove with a slotted spoon and set aside.

Add a little extra oil to the pan if necessary, and fry the onion, garlic, bell pepper, potatoes and fennel seeds for 10 minutes. Add the tomatoes, wine, bay leaves and thyme, bring to a boil, and boil rapidly for 5 minutes until reduced. Cover and simmer gently for 10 minutes.

Return the fish and mushrooms to the pan, cover and simmer for a further 20 minutes until the fish is cooked.

Sprinkle over the chopped thyme, and serve with mashed potatoes or bread to soak up the juices.

Top: SOUPE AUX POISSONS
Bottom: FISH STEWED IN RED WINE

SMOKED FISH CHOWDER

Serves 6

A recent trip to Seattle introduced me to the ingenious method of serving fish chowder in hollowed-out bread rolls. You will need to use large crusty rolls, served in soup bowls.

6 large crisp bread rolls	2½ cups milk
2 tbsp butter	1 large potato, diced
1 cup diced smoked bacon	8 ounces undyed smoked
1 onion, chopped	haddock or cod, skinned
1 celery stalk, sliced	⅔ cup light cream (optional)
1 small red bell pepper, seeded	2 tbsp chopped fresh chives
and diced	Pinch of cayenne pepper
1¼ cups vegetable stock	Salt and pepper

Preheat the oven to 400°F. Cut the tops from each roll, scoop out and discard the middle, leaving the outer crust intact to act as a bowl. Bake in the oven for 8-10 minutes until crisp, place each roll in a soup bowl, and set aside.

Melt the butter in a large pan, and fry the bacon for 4-5 minutes until browned. Add the onion, celery and pepper, and fry for 5 minutes. Add the stock, milk and potato. Bring to a boil, cover and simmer for 10 minutes.

Cut the fish into bite-size pieces, add to the pan, and simmer for a further 10 minutes until the fish and potato are cooked.

Stir in the cream (if using), the chives and cayenne, and heat through for 1 minute. Adjust the seasoning, and spoon the chowder into the rolls.

CRAB BISQUE

Serves 4-6

A delicious creamy puréed soup of fresh crab meat and butternut squash with a subtle hint of fresh ginger.

2 tbsp butter	1 quart vegetable or chicken
1 onion, chopped	stock
2 celery stalks, chopped	Cayenne pepper
2 tsp grated ginger root	Salt and pepper
1 pound butternut squash,	**GARNISH**
chopped	Croûtons
⅔ cup dry white wine	Freshly grated Parmesan cheese
12 ounces fresh crab meat	

Melt the butter in a large pan, and fry the onion, celery and ginger root for 5 minutes. Add the squash, and fry for a further 5 minutes.

Pour in the wine, and boil rapidly for 3 minutes, then stir in the crab meat, stock and cayenne pepper, bring to a boil, cover and simmer for 20 minutes.

Transfer the soup to a blender and purée until smooth. Return to the pan, reheat for 2 minutes, and season to taste. Serve the soup hot, garnished with the reserved crab meat, croûtons and freshly grated Parmesan.

Top: SMOKED FISH CHOWDER
Bottom: CRAB BISQUE

HOT AND SOUR THAI FISH SOUP

Serves 6

One of the most famous of all Thai soups, with an exquisite combination of sweet, sour and hot.

1 pound raw shrimp in shells	2 small green chilies, seeded and chopped
1 onion, sliced	4 cilantro roots, washed and finely chopped (see page 80)
2 slices fresh ginger root	18 fresh small mussels, scrubbed
2 stalks lemon grass, crushed	
2 kaffir lime leaves, sliced, or 1 tbsp grated lime zest	2 tbsp light soy sauce
1½ quarts vegetable stock	6 small squid, cleaned (see pages 6-7) and cut into rings
1 tbsp sunflower oil	
1 tsp sesame oil	1 carrot, cut into matchsticks
2 garlic cloves, crushed	1 cup watercress

Prepare the stock: peel the shrimp, reserve the flesh, and place the shells and heads in a large pan. Add the onion, ginger root, lemon grass, lime leaves or zest and the stock. Bring to a boil, cover and simmer for 30 minutes. Strain into a clean pan.

Heat the sunflower oil and sesame oil in a small pan. Add the garlic, chilies and cilantro root, and fry for 3 minutes until softened. Purée in a blender to form a smooth paste, and set aside.

Place the mussels in a pan with just the water left on the shells after scrubbing. Steam for 4-5 minutes until the shells have opened. Discard any that remain closed. Pour the liquid through a fine strainer into a bowl, whisk in the garlic paste, and stir into the strained lemon grass stock. Allow the mussels to cool slightly, remove from their shells and set aside.

Add the shrimp and squid to the stock, simmer for 5 minutes, then add the carrot. Simmer for 3 minutes, and finally add the cooked mussels and watercress leaves. Heat through for a further minute, and serve at once.

COCONUT FISH SOUP

Serves 6

The classic Thai ingredients of lemon grass, lime leaves, ginger and coconut lend a truly authentic flavor to this rich fish soup.

2 stalks lemon grass, halved and lightly crushed	1 tsp ground turmeric
	14-ounce can coconut milk
4 slices fresh ginger root	1¼ pounds mixed fish fillets (e.g. cod, monkfish, flounder and hake)
4 kaffir lime leaves, shredded or 1 tbsp grated lime zest	
2 tbsp chopped fresh cilantro	2 tbsp light soy sauce
1 quart vegetable stock or water	GARNISH
1 tbsp sunflower oil	Sesame oil
1 onion, finely chopped	Lime juice
1 green chili, seeded and chopped	Fresh cilantro leaves

Place the lemon grass, ginger root, lime leaves or grated zest and cilantro in a pan. Add half the stock or water, bring to a boil, cover and simmer gently for 30 minutes. Remove from the heat, and set aside.

Heat the oil in a large pan and fry the onion, chili and turmeric for 5 minutes. Add the coconut milk, remaining stock, fish fillets and soy sauce, and bring to a boil. Lower the heat, and simmer very gently for 5-8 minutes until the fish is tender. Using a slotted spoon, transfer the fish to warmed soup bowls.

Strain the lemon grass stock into the coconut stock, bring to a boil, and simmer for 5 minutes.

Pour the stock over the fish, and serve at once, drizzled with a little sesame oil and lime juice, and garnished with cilantro leaves.

Top: HOT AND SOUR THAI FISH SOUP
Bottom: COCONUT FISH SOUP

TOMATO SOUP WITH FISH QUENELLES

Serves 6

Quenelles are made from a mousse-like mixture of puréed fish, cream and egg whites, which is then shaped into ovals and lightly poached. It is important to keep the mixture as cool as possible to achieve a light fluffy texture.

2 tbsp olive oil	2 tbsp chopped fresh basil
1 onion, chopped	Fresh basil leaves, to garnish
2 garlic cloves, crushed	**QUENELLES**
2 pounds ripe tomatoes, chopped	8 ounces smoked cod fillet
	Grated zest of ½ lemon
1 tbsp chopped fresh parsley	Salt and pepper
2 tsp chopped fresh thyme	2 small egg whites
⅔ cup dry white wine	⅓ cup light cream
1¼ cups chicken or vegetable stock	

Prepare the quenelles: skin and remove any bones from the cod, and purée in a blender with the lemon zest and plenty of seasoning until very smooth. Blend in the egg whites, and transfer to a bowl. Half-fill a larger bowl with ice, and sit the bowl of fish purée on top. Gradually beat in the cream, a little at a time. Chill for 2 hours.

To make the soup: heat the oil in a pan, and fry the onion and garlic for 5 minutes. Add the tomatoes, parsley, thyme and wine, and boil rapidly for 5 minutes. Add the stock, cover and simmer for 30 minutes. Purée the soup, pass through a strainer into a pan, and stir in the basil.

To cook the quenelles: bring a large pan of water to a steady simmer. Form the chilled fish purée into ovals by passing the mixture from one spoon to another to make egg-shaped mousses. Poach the quenelles in the gently simmering water for about 1 minute, or until they rise to the surface. Drain on paper towels.

Quickly reheat the soup, and serve each portion topped with 3 quenelles, garnished with basil leaves.

MUSSEL AND SCALLOP SOUP WITH CHIVES

Serves 4

A lovely soup perfect for special guests at a dinner party. The more flavor you get from the fish stock, the more delicious the end result will be.

12 fresh scallops, cleaned	⅔ pint dry white wine
2 tbsp unsalted butter	6 white peppercorns
2 small leeks, shredded	2½ cups Fish Stock
20 fresh mussels, scrubbed	(see page 7)
1 onion, chopped	⅔ cup light cream
2 sprigs parsley	2 tbsp chopped fresh chives

Separate the scallops from their corals, cut the white flesh in half, and set aside.

Melt half the butter in a small pan, and fry the leeks for 2 minutes until softened. Transfer to serving bowls, and keep warm while preparing the soup.

Put the mussels, onion, parsley, wine and peppercorns in a large pan, and steam for 4-5 minutes until all the mussel shells are opened. Discard any that remain closed. Allow to cool slightly, then carefully remove the mussels from their shells, and set aside.

Pour the cooking liquid through a fine strainer into a clean pan, add the fish stock, bring to a boil, and simmer until reduced by half.

Add the scallops to the stock, and simmer for 2 minutes, then add the cooked mussels, and heat through. Using a slotted spoon, transfer the shellfish to the soup bowls, and arrange on top of the leeks.

Stir the cream and chives into the stock, and boil rapidly until reduced slightly. Season to taste, and pour into the bowls. Serve immediately.

Top Right: TOMATO SOUP WITH FISH QUENELLES
Bottom Left: MUSSEL AND SCALLOP SOUP WITH CHIVES

APPETIZERS
AND STARTERS

*T*HIS SECOND CHAPTER *is full of exciting ideas to serve as pre-dinner nibbles to stimulate the appetite, delicious for a dinner party, or even a light lunch or snack meal.* Tapenade *and* Anchoïade *spread on crispy garlic bread and topped with broiled bell peppers, tomatoes and cheese make a stunning plate of tasty hors d'oeuvre. This particular dish is one of my favorites and is always popular with my guests.*

I find starters are often the most tempting dishes, so I have tried to include a varied selection, inspired by cuisines from all around the world. They include many classics that I have enjoyed on travels and have adapted for this book, including the Stuffed Filo Shrimp Fingers, *a Goan speciality, and the equally delicious Italian antipasti,* Fresh Tuna and Bean Salad.

CONTENTS

BROILED HERRING TOASTS

Serves 6

A quick and easy toasted sandwich, this makes a perfect brunch or light lunch.

≈≈

6 medium herrings, filleted	*1 tbsp chopped fresh tarragon*
6 large slices of bread	*Lemon juice*
1 tbsp wholegrain mustard	*Salt and pepper*
¼ cup butter	*Sour cream or yogurt, to serve*

≈≈

Preheat the broiler. Cut the herring fillets through the back, and using a small pair of tweezers, pull out any larger bones. Lightly toast the bread on both sides.

Cream the mustard, butter and tarragon together, and spread a little over 1 side of the toasted bread. Place 2 halved herring fillets on each slice, trimming the fillets to the size of the bread. Spread over the remaining mustard butter.

Squeeze a little lemon juice over each one, season, and return to the broiler for 5-6 minutes until the fish is cooked through.

Serve at once with sour cream or yogurt, if wished.

SMOKED MACKEREL AND ORANGE PATE

Serves 4

As you bite into this tangy pâté the delicious green peppercorns explode in the mouth, adding both texture and a fiery flavor.

≈≈

8 ounces smoked mackerel fillet, skinned and boned	*Squeeze of lemon juice*
2 tbsp butter, softened	*⅔ cup low-fat cream cheese*
2 tbsp freshly squeezed orange juice	*1 tbsp green peppercorns*
2 tbsp cointreau or orange juice	*Lightly crushed Melba toast, French bread or vegetable crudités, to serve*
2 tbsp chopped fresh chives	

≈≈

Place the mackerel in a bowl, and mash well with a fork. Beat in the remaining ingredients to form a fairly coarse paste. Transfer to a bowl, cover and chill for 1 hour.

Remove the pâté from the refrigerator at least 30 minutes before serving to return to room temperature. Serve with Melba toast, French bread or a selection of vegetable crudités.

Top: BROILED HERRING TOASTS
Bottom: SMOKED MACKEREL AND ORANGE PATE

WARM SMOKED FISH MOUSSE

Serves 4

The flavor of smoked fish, combined with a light texture, makes these mousses a perfect dinner party starter.

1 pound undyed smoked fish, skinned and boned	**TOMATO VINAIGRETTE**
Grated zest of ½ lemon	*2 tbsp olive oil*
1 tbsp cognac	*4 ripe tomatoes, peeled, seeded and diced*
3 egg whites	*2 shallots, finely chopped*
2 tbsp chopped fresh tarragon	*1 tbsp shredded fresh basil*
2 tsp hot horseradish sauce	*Juice of ½ lemon*
White pepper	*Salt and pepper*
⅔ cup light cream	*Fresh herbs, to garnish*

Cube the smoked fish, place in a blender with the lemon zest and cognac, and purée until very smooth. Transfer to a bowl, and gradually beat in the egg whites, tarragon, horseradish and pepper. Cover and chill for 2 hours.

Preheat the oven to 350°F. Half-fill a roasting pan with boiling water, and place on the middle shelf of the oven. Remove the fish purée from the refrigerator, and sit the bowl in a larger bowl filled with crushed ice. Gradually whisk in the cream until incorporated, and spoon into 4 greased ramekin dishes.

Place the ramekins in the roasting pan, and bake for 25-30 minutes until mousses are risen and firm to the touch. Remove from the oven, and leave to rest for 5 minutes.

Meanwhile, prepare the vinaigrette: heat the oil in a small pan, stir in the tomatoes, shallots and basil, and heat gently for 5 minutes. Remove from the heat and whisk in the lemon juice and seasonings. Keep warm.

Unmold the mousses onto individual plates, pour over a little of the tomato vinaigrette, and serve at once, garnished with basil or tarragon sprigs.

BAKED STUFFED TOMATOES

Serves 6

Tomatoes and crab combine well together. Here the tomatoes are stuffed with a mixture of crab meat and bread crumbs, and baked until soft and golden.

6 beef tomatoes	*2 cups fresh white bread crumbs*
3 tbsp olive oil	*2 tbsp chopped fresh parsley*
1 small onion, finely chopped	*1 tbsp wholegrain mustard*
1 garlic clove, crushed	*½ cup freshly grated Parmesan cheese*
8 ounces fresh white crabmeat	*Salt and pepper*

Preheat the oven to 400°F. Cut the tops from the tomatoes, and carefully scoop out the flesh. Chop finely and reserve.

Heat the oil in a frying pan, and fry the onion and garlic for 5 minutes until browned. Stir in the chopped tomato, crabmeat, bread crumbs, parsley, mustard, and two-thirds of the cheese. Season to taste.

Spoon the filling into the hollowed-out tomato shells, piling the mixture up.

Transfer the tomatoes to a baking dish, sprinkle over the remaining cheese, drizzle with a little extra olive oil and bake for 40 minutes until softened and the filling brown. Serve at once with a crisp green salad.

Top: WARM SMOKED FISH MOUSSE
Bottom: BAKED STUFFED TOMATOES

SALT COD FRITTERS WITH GARLIC SAUCE

Serves 8-12

These tasty salt cod fritters remind me of glorious sunny days in Greece. The fritters can be cooked ahead of time and crisped up in a hot oven, just before serving.

2 pounds salt cod	4 tbsp water
Milk	2 garlic cloves, chopped
BATTER	1 tbsp lemon juice
1 cup all-purpose flour	Pinch of cayenne pepper
1 tsp salt	6 tbsp olive oil
1 scant cup milk	Vegetable oil, for deep frying
2 tbsp ouzo or brandy	4 tbsp all-purpose flour
1 egg, lightly beaten	**GARNISH**
2 tbsp chopped fresh cilantro	Lemon wedges
GARLIC SAUCE	Fresh cilantro sprigs
2-3 slices of stale white bread, crusts removed	

Prepare the salt cod (see page 14).

Make the batter: sift the flour and salt into a large bowl, and make a well in the center. Gradually beat in the milk, ouzo or brandy and egg to form a smooth pouring batter. Stir in the cilantro, and let rest for 30 minutes.

Meanwhile, make the garlic sauce: pour the water over the bread, and soak for 5 minutes. Squeeze out the water, place the bread, garlic, lemon juice and cayenne in a blender, and purée to form a thick paste. Gradually work in the oil, a little at a time, to form a thick sauce, thinning with 2-3 tbsp boiling water if the sauce is too thick. Transfer to a bowl, cover and set aside.

To fry: heat the oil in a deep, heavy-based pan to 350°F, or until a cube of bread browns in 30 seconds. Dust the cubes of salt cod with a little seasoned flour, dip in the batter, and deep-fry in batches for 4-5 minutes until crisp and golden. Drain on paper towels.

Serve with the garlic sauce.

CLARE'S STUFFED BELL PEPPERS

Serves 6

Although this is a version of a classic Italian dish from Piedmont, I have named it after a friend who always cooks the bell peppers to perfection.

2-ounce can anchovies in oil, drained	3 large ripe tomatoes, peeled and quartered
Milk	Salt and pepper
1 garlic clove, crushed	6 tbsp olive oil
1 tbsp chopped fresh basil	1 tbsp balsamic vinegar
3 bell peppers, red, yellow or orange	Fresh basil sprigs, to garnish

Preheat the oven to 425°F. Place the anchovy fillets in a small dish, cover with milk, and let soak for 10 minutes. Drain, wash well and pat dry. Chop finely, and mix with the garlic and basil.

Cut the bell peppers in half through the stalks. Scoop out the seeds, and arrange in a roasting pan, cut side up.

Place 2 tomato quarters in each pepper half, and divide the anchovy mixture between the peppers. Season well.

Whisk together the oil and vinegar, pour into the peppers, and bake for about 1 hour until golden and caramelized.

Serve hot, garnished with basil, or let cool to room temperature, and serve with a salad and crisp French bread to mop up the juices.

Top: SALT COD FRITTERS WITH GARLIC SAUCE

SOLE FILLETS WITH WARM CAPER DRESSING

Serves 4

All credit must go to my dear friend Judy Ridgway, who served a version of this wonderful dish to me at a memorable dinner party.

~~

2 medium sole, skinned, filleted and cut in half lengthways	1 tbsp chopped fresh dillweed
	4 sun-dried tomatoes in oil, drained and sliced
4 tbsp dry white wine	Grated zest of ½ orange
2 tbsp orange juice	2 tsp balsamic or red wine vinegar
Salt and pepper	
6 tbsp olive oil	Corn salad, to garnish
4 tbsp drained capers, washed and dried	

~~

Preheat the oven to 425°F. Roll up each halved sole fillet, secure with toothpicks, and arrange in a baking dish in a single layer.

Add the wine and orange juice, season well, cover with foil, and bake for 20 minutes or until the sole is cooked through, feeling firm to the touch.

Meanwhile, heat half the oil in a small pan, and stir in the capers, dillweed, tomatoes and orange zest. Heat gently until almost boiling, remove from the heat and keep warm.

Strain the fish juices from the sole fillets into the pan with the capers. Cover the sole fillets with foil to keep warm. Bring the sauce to a boil, whisk in the remaining oil and the vinegar, and simmer for 1 minute.

Arrange 2 sole fillets on each plate, pour over the warm dressing, and serve at once, garnished with the salad leaves.

CELERIAC ROSTIS WITH SMOKED SALMON

Serves 4

Celeriac is used here instead of the more traditional potato, to make mouth-watering rostis. Topped with smoked salmon and sour cream they make a delicious dinner party starter.

~~

2½ cups peeled and grated celeriac	1 egg, lightly beaten
½ small onion, very thinly sliced	Oil for shallow frying
	8 ounces smoked salmon
1 tbsp chopped fresh chives	4 tbsp sour cream or natural yogurt
½ tsp salt	Salt and pepper
1 tsp grated fresh horseradish	Chopped fresh chives, to garnish
1½ tbsp self-rising flour	

~~

Place the grated celeriac in a large bowl, and stir in the onion, chives, salt, horseradish and flour. Beat in the egg until evenly combined.

Heat about ½-inch oil in a non-stick skillet. Divide the celeriac mixture into 8, spoon half into the hot oil, pressing each one flat to make a small pancake or rosti. Fry for 3-4 minutes on each side until crisp and golden. Drain on paper towels, and keep warm while cooking the remaining mixture.

Place 2 rostis on each plate. Top with the salmon and a spoonful of sour cream, and garnish with chopped chives.

Top: CELERIAC ROSTIS WITH SMOKED SALMON
Bottom: SOLE FILLETS WITH WARM CAPER DRESSING

TAPENADE AND ANCHOIADE CROSTINI

Serves 4 - 8

These tangy spreads make delicious toppings for crostini or bruschetta. Both mixtures can be prepared ahead of time, and stored in a sealed jar in the refrigerator for several weeks.

≈

TAPENADE
2-ounce can anchovies in oil, drained
Milk
¾ cup pitted black olives
2 tbsp drained capers, washed
1 garlic clove, crushed
1 tsp grated lemon zest
2 tbsp chopped fresh parsley
4 tbsp light olive oil
ANCHOIADE
2 x 2-ounce cans anchovies in oil, drained
Milk
2 garlic cloves, crushed
2 tbsp chopped fresh basil
2 tsp lemon juice
¼ cup almonds, toasted and ground

4 tbsp olive oil
Salt and pepper
CROSTINI
8 thick slices ciabatta or rustic French bread
2 garlic cloves
olive oil, to drizzle
TOPPINGS
Topping 1: broiled bell peppers, goat cheese and arugula leaves
Topping 2: sliced plum tomatoes, crushed garlic, basil leaves
Topping 3: broiled Belgian chicory halves
Topping 4: broiled fennel slices

≈

For the tapenade: soak the anchovy fillets in milk for 10 minutes. Drain, wash well, and pat dry.

Roughly chop the anchovies, and combine with the remaining ingredients. Pound in a mortar or purée in a blender to form a fairly smooth paste. Cover and set aside.

For the anchoiade: prepare as for tapenade.

For the crostini: toast the bread lightly on both sides, rub all over with garlic, and then drizzle with olive oil.

Spread either the tapenade or anchoiade over one side of each slice. Top with any of the suggested toppings, return to the broiler for a few seconds, and serve immediately.

FRESH TUNA AND BEAN SALAD

Serves 4

The wonderful flavor and texture of fresh tuna is worth the extra expense, as it transforms this dish into a very memorable salad.

≈

1 pound fresh tuna steak, cubed
4 tbsp olive oil
1 garlic clove, crushed
14-ounce can flageolet or white kidney beans, drained
1 red onion, thinly sliced

2 ripe plum tomatoes, peeled, seeded and diced
2 tbsp chopped fresh parsley
1 tbsp chopped fresh basil
2 tsp balsamic vinegar
Salt and pepper
2 cups arugula or salad leaves

≈

Heat half the oil in a skillet, add the tuna, cover and fry over a low heat for 4-5 minutes until cooked – it should still be a little pink in the center.

Transfer the fish and all the pan juices to a large bowl, and stir in the garlic, beans, onion, tomatoes and herbs.

Blend the remaining oil with the vinegar and seasonings, pour over the salad, toss well, and leave to marinate for 1 hour. Stir in the arugula or salad leaves, and serve immediately.

Top: FRESH TUNA AND BEAN SALAD
Bottom: TAPENADE AND ANCHOIADE CROSTINI

STUFFED FILO SHRIMP FINGERS

Serves 4

I tasted a similar dish to these shrimp fingers in Goa, where the shrimp were wrapped in soft poppadoms and fried. I have substituted filo pastry with great success.

2 scallions, finely chopped	3 sheets filo pastry
1 tbsp chopped fresh cilantro	2 tbsp olive oil
1 garlic clove, crushed	12 cooked jumbo shrimp,
1 tsp grated fresh ginger root	shelled and de-veined (see
1 small fresh red chili, seeded	pages 6-7)
and chopped	Vegetable oil, for deep frying
1 tsp tamarind paste or	Chili Soy Dip, to serve
lemon juice	(optional)
1 tbsp tomato paste	

Place the scallions, cilantro, garlic, ginger root, chili, tamarind paste or lemon juice and tomato paste in a blender, and purée to form a smooth paste.

Cut each sheet of pastry lengthways into four 8- x 3-inch strips. Take one strip and brush with a little of the oil, spread ½ tsp of the chili paste along one narrow end, and place a shrimp over the top, with only the tail extending beyond the edge of the pastry. Roll up to enclose the shrimp, twisting the ends together to seal. Cover with a clean dish cloth and repeat to make 12 fingers.

Heat 4 inches oil in a heavy-based pan to a temperature of 350°F, or until a cube of bread browns in 30 seconds. Carefully slip in the shrimp fingers, and cook for 2 minutes until the pastry is crisp and golden.

Drain on paper towels, and serve at once with the chili soy dip (see opposite).

THAI SHRIMP WITH CHILI SOY DIP

Serves 4 - 6

These crispy Thai-style shrimp balls are delicious dipped into the chili soy sauce.

12 ounces cooked peeled shrimp	2 tbsp all-purpose flour
1 cup fresh bread crumbs	1 egg, beaten
½ small onion, very finely	⅔ cup shredded coconut
chopped	Vegetable oil, for deep-frying
1 garlic clove, crushed	DIP
1 tbsp chopped fresh cilantro	1 small red chili, seeded and
Grated zest and juice	sliced
of ½ lime	1 tbsp lime juice
1 small green chili, seeded	2 tbsp dark soy sauce
and chopped	2 tbsp water
¼ tsp five-spice powder	1 tbsp soft brown sugar

Place the shrimp, bread crumbs, onion, garlic, cilantro, lime juice and zest, chili and spice in a blender, and purée to form a smooth paste. Chill for 30 minutes.

Divide the shrimp mixture into 12 and roll each piece into small balls. Dust lightly with flour, and dip into the egg, and then the coconut, to completely coat the balls. Chill for a further 30 minutes.

Meanwhile, prepare the dip: place all the ingredients in a small pan, and heat gently to dissolve the sugar. Set aside to cool.

Heat the oil in a heavy-based pan, and fry the balls in batches for 3-4 minutes until crisp and golden. Drain on paper towels, and keep warm while frying the remaining balls. Serve hot with the dip.

Top: STUFFED FILO SHRIMP FINGERS
Bottom: THAI SHRIMP BALLS WITH CHILI SOY DIP

JAPANESE SHRIMP TEMPURA

Serves 6

To insure the batter for the shrimp is light and crispy, make it at the last minute and do not overbeat the mixture – it should be slightly lumpy. For the dipping sauce, use tamari, which is the slightly thicker type of soy sauce.

30 large raw shrimp in shells	2 tbsp grated daikon
DIPPING SAUCE	vegetable oil, for deep frying
2 tbsp tamari soy sauce	**BATTER**
2 tbsp lemon juice	1 large egg
2 tbsp sake or sweet sherry	1 cup all-purpose flour, sifted
1 tsp clear honey	⅔ cup cold water
1 scallion, shredded	

Remove the head and shells from the shrimp, and cut out the vein from the back of the shrimp. Wash and pat dry. Combine the ingredients for the sauce, and set aside.

To make the batter: lightly beat the egg until the yolk is broken and starting to blend with the white. Stir in the flour and then the water, until just combined. Do not overmix the batter; there should still be a few lumps in the mixture. Set the batter bowl in a larger bowl filled with ice cubes.

Heat about 4 inches of oil in a deep heavy-based pan to a temperature of 350°F on a sugar thermometer, or until a cube of bread browns in 30 seconds.

Holding the shrimp by the tails, dip into the batter, and then carefully slip them into the hot oil. Fry the shrimp five at a time for about 2 minutes until the batter is golden and very crisp. Drain on paper towels, and keep warm while frying the remaining shrimp.

Serve at once with the dipping sauce.

SCALLOPS WITH BLACK BEAN SAUCE

Serves 4

Fermented black beans are available in cans from Oriental stores. Wash several times in cold water to extract the excess saltiness.

12 fresh scallops on the shell	2 tsp grated fresh ginger root
2 tbsp fermented black beans	4 tbsp light soy sauce
2 scallions, thinly sliced	2 tbsp dry sherry
½ red bell pepper, seeded and thinly sliced	Juice of 1 lemon

Carefully remove the scallops from the shells by snipping through the muscle that attaches them. Wash and reserve the shells. Wash the scallops, pat dry, and place in a shallow dish.

Wash the beans well, and add to the dish with the remaining ingredients except the lemon juice. Cover and marinate for at least 1 hour.

Transfer the scallops and their marinade to a heatproof plate and pour over the lemon juice. Set a trivet in a large pan with about 1 inch of water, and bring to a boil. Place the plate on the trivet, cover the pan with a lid, and simmer gently for 3-4 minutes until the scallops are just tender.

Return the scallops to their shells with all the cooking liquid, and serve immediately.

Top: JAPANESE SHRIMP TEMPURA
Bottom: SCALLOPS WITH BLACK BEAN SAUCE

CRAWFISH WITH THREE DIPS

Serves 4

Serve as a starter, with one or all three dips as accompaniments. Use fresh jumbo shrimp if you cannot find crawfish.

20-24 fresh crawfish	½ tsp paprika
Lemon wedges, to garnish	Pinch of cayenne pepper
PEPPER DIP	¼ cup olive oil
½ red bell pepper, halved	1 tbsp balsamic vinegar
and seeded	2 tbsp boiling water
1 small garlic clove, crushed	**SESAME AND**
2 tbsp olive oil	**GINGER DIP**
Yolk of 1 hard-cooked egg,	¼ cup mayonnaise
chopped	1 tsp sesame oil
1 tbsp chopped fresh parsley	1 tsp grated fresh ginger root
SPICED DIP	1 tsp orange juice
1 garlic clove, crushed	Pinch of five-spice powder
½ tsp cumin seeds, toasted	

Wash and dry the crawfish. Bring a large pan of water to a rolling boil, plunge in the crawfish, return to a boil, and poach for 3 minutes. Drain, refresh briefly under cold running water, and leave to go cold.

Meanwhile, prepare the dips. For the bell pepper dip, broil the pepper for 5 minutes on each side until charred and softened. Cool, peel, and discard the skin. Purée the flesh in a blender, then gradually blend in the remaining ingredients to form a smooth sauce. Cover and set aside.

For the spiced dip, place the crushed garlic and spices in a grinder, and blend to form a fairly smooth paste. Transfer to a bowl and very gradually whisk in the oil, then the vinegar, and finally the water, to form a thin pouring consistency. Cover and set aside.

For the sesame and ginger dip, combine all the ingredients in a bowl until evenly blended. Cover and set aside.

Serve the poached crawfish on a large platter with the 3 dips. Garnish and serve with French bread.

SCALLOP AND PROSCIUTTO KEBABS

Serves 4

The salsa for the kebabs can be made ahead and kept in the refrigerator for several hours.

20 large fresh scallops	**SALSA**
10 thin slices prosciutto	1 ripe mango, peeled, stoned
20 large sage leaves	and diced
Selection of salad greens, to	2 ripe tomatoes, peeled, seeded
serve	and diced
MARINADE	1 fresh green chili, seeded and
2 tbsp chopped fresh chervil	diced
1 tsp fennel seeds, toasted and	2 tbsp chopped fresh chervil
crushed	½ red onion, finely chopped
2 sprigs rosemary	Juice of 1 lime
⅔ cup dry white wine	2 tbsp hazelnut oil
4 tbsp hazelnut oil	½ tsp sugar
	Salt and pepper

Wash the scallops. Cut away the tough gray membrane from each one, and pat dry.

Cut each slice of prosciutto in half lengthways to form 20 long thin strips.

Wrap a sage leaf, and then a strip of ham around each scallop, to form small packages. Thread onto 4 skewers and place in a shallow dish.

Combine the marinade ingredients, and pour over the kebabs. Cover and marinate for 2 hours.

Meanwhile, make the salsa: combine all the ingredients, season to taste, and set aside for the flavors to infuse.

Preheat the broiler. Remove the scallop packages from their marinade, brush with the marinade and broil for 2-3 minutes on each side until charred and firm to the touch.

Serve the kebabs at once, with a little salsa and a selection of salad greens.

Top: SCALLOP AND PROSCIUTTO KEBABS
Bottom: CRAWFISH WITH THREE DIPS

MARINATED HERRING SALAD

Serves 4

A typical Scandinavian recipe using raw herring which is marinated in lemon juice to "cook" the flesh and then served with a beet and apple salad.

1 pound very fresh herring, filleted	*½ tsp creamed horseradish*
Juice of 4 lemons	*2 tsp chopped fresh tarragon*
1 cup diced cooked beets	*Salt and pepper*
1 eating apple, cored and diced	**GARNISH**
¾ cup diced cucumber	*Radicchio leaves*
2 tbsp sour cream	*Sliced red onion*

Wash and dry the herring fillets. Using a pair of fine tweezers, pull out any small bones. Place the fillets skin-side down in a large shallow dish, to fit in a single layer. Pour over the lemon juice, cover and refrigerate overnight. Allow the fish to return to room temperature for about 1 hour before serving.

Mix together the beet, apple, cucumber, sour cream, horseradish, tarragon, seasonings, and 1 tbsp of the herring marinade. Set aside to infuse for 1 hour.

Remove the herring fillets from the marinade, and cut into bite-size pieces.

Arrange the fillets on plates with a spoonful of the beet relish, and garnish with radicchio leaves and slices of red onion.

CARPACCIO WITH AVOCADO SALSA

Serves 6

You will need a very sharp knife to cut the raw haddock into wafer thin slices so that it can "cook" in the citrus marinade.

1½ pounds very fresh haddock fillet	**AVOCADO SALSA**
Grated zest of 1 lime	*½ onion, finely chopped*
Juice of 3 limes	*2 ripe tomatoes, peeled, seeded and diced*
1 fresh green chili, seeded and sliced	*1 ripe avocado, peeled, pitted and diced*
4 scallions, sliced	*Juice of ½ lime*
1 tsp coriander seeds, crushed	*1 garlic clove, crushed*
2 sprigs fresh thyme	*Pinch of salt*
4 sprigs fresh chervil	*Pinch of sugar*
6 tbsp olive oil	*2 tbsp chopped fresh cilantro*
	1 tbsp olive oil

Wash and dry the haddock and pull out any remaining bones. Using a very sharp knife, cut the fish on an angle into paper-thin slices, and place in a shallow dish.

Combine all the remaining ingredients, pour over the fish, and marinate for 1 hour at room temperature.

Meanwhile, prepare the salsa: mix all the ingredients together, cover and set aside.

Remove the haddock from its marinade, and arrange on plates with a spoonful of the salsa.

Top: MARINATED HERRING SALAD
Bottom: HADDOCK CARPACCIO WITH AVOCADO SALSA

SIMPLE FAMILY DISHES

MOST OF US *today have busy schedules and hectic lifestyles so fish provides the perfect answer, as it generally cooks quickly. The recipes in this chapter are ideal for midweek family meals; they take a minimum amount of time to prepare and use fish that is readily available. Pasta and seafood make a delicious combination and I have included several simple family recipes here. Both the* Spaghetti Vongole *and* Pasta with Mussels in Herb Sauce *take only minutes to prepare, while the* Pasta with Smoked Salmon *offers another quick dish for a special treat.*

The lighter recipes, such as Spanish Style Shrimp *and* Steamed Mussels with Ginger and Cilantro*, make great light lunches and, again, are simple to make and ready to eat in minutes.*

CONTENTS

≈

SEAFOOD PIZZA

Serves 2

These individual pizzas, topped with mixed
seafood, taste as tantalizing as they look. Served
with a crisp green salad they make the perfect
light lunch dish.

2 cups strong bread flour
½ tsp easy-blend yeast
¼ tsp salt
6 tbsp tepid water
1 tbsp olive oil

SAUCE

1 tbsp olive oil
1 garlic clove, chopped
4 large tomatoes, peeled,
seeded and chopped
1 tbsp tomato paste
2 tsp chopped fresh oregano
2 tsp chopped fresh basil

TOPPING

2-ounce can anchovies in oil,
drained
Milk, for soaking
12 fresh mussels, scrubbed
1 tbsp olive oil
10 raw jumbo shrimp, shelled
and deveined (see pages 6-7)
2 small squid, cleaned (see
pages 6-7), sliced into rings
8 ounces mozzarella cheese,
thinly sliced
10 black olives
A few basil leaves, shredded
Basil sprigs, to garnish

Make the pizza dough: combine the flour, yeast and salt in a large bowl. Make a well in the center, and work in the water and oil to form a firm dough. Transfer to a lightly floured surface, and knead for 8-10 minutes until smooth and elastic. Place the dough in an oiled bowl, cover and leave to rise in a warm place for 45 minutes, or until doubled in size.

Meanwhile, prepare the sauce: heat the oil in a small pan, fry the garlic for 2 minutes until golden, then add the remaining ingredients. Bring to a boil, cover and simmer gently for 15 minutes. Remove the lid, and simmer for a further 10 minutes until thickened. Leave to cool.

Prepare the topping: soak the anchovies in milk for 10 minutes. Drain, wash well and pat dry.

Steam the mussels in a little water for 3-4 minutes until the shells have opened. Discard any that remain closed. Cool slightly, and remove from their shells, reserving 4 for garnish.

Heat the oil in a large pan, and quickly fry the shrimp and squid for 1 minute until lightly browned.

Preheat the oven to 475°F and lightly oil two 8-inch shallow cake pans. Place a large baking sheet on the top shelf of the oven.

Knead the risen dough, divide in half, and roll each one into a round to fit into the prepared pans. Spread each round with a little tomato sauce, and top with the sliced mozzarella, prepared seafood, olives, and a few basil leaves.

Transfer to the hot baking sheets, and cook for 18-20 minutes until risen and golden. Serve immediately, garnished with the reserved mussels, and sprigs of basil.

SMOKED HADDOCK PILAF

Serves 6-8

Rice and fish make a great combination, and the two work well together in this spicy Middle Eastern pilaf.

1 pound smoked haddock fillets	½ tsp ground cumin
2½ cups Court Bouillon (see pages 6-7)	½ tsp ground mixed spice
	⅓ cup raisins
1¼ cups basmati rice	½ cup cashew nuts, toasted
1 tsp salt	1 tbsp chopped fresh mint
2 tbsp olive oil	2 tbsp butter (optional)
8 ounces baby onions, halved if large	Pepper
	GARNISH
1 tsp ground coriander	2 hard-cooked eggs, quartered
	Mint sprigs

Wash and dry the haddock. Place in a large wide pan with the court bouillon, and bring to a boil. Simmer for about 3 minutes, until the fish starts to flake. Remove the fish with a slotted spoon, and drain on paper towels. Discard the skin and any bones, and flake the flesh. Reserve the stock.

Meanwhile, place the rice into a bowl with the salt. Cover with warm water, leave to cool, and then drain.

Preheat the oven to 400°F, and lightly oil a large baking dish.

Fry the onions in the olive oil for 5 minutes, add the rice and spices, and stir-fry for 2 minutes.

Reheat the fish stock until boiling, and stir into the rice with the raisins and nuts. Bring to a boil, cover and simmer for 12 minutes, until the rice has absorbed most of the liquid. Stir in the mint, and remove from the heat.

Spoon one-third of the rice mixture into the baking dish, arrange half of the flaked haddock over the top and repeat, finishing with the rice. Cover with foil, and bake for 20 minutes. Stir in the butter, garnish and serve.

BAKED MACKEREL WITH LEMONS AND SPICES

Serves 4

A Middle Eastern-style dish, in which the lemon and spices complement the richness of the fish.

4 medium mackerel, cleaned	4 tbsp olive oil
2 lemons, sliced	1 tsp paprika
2 sprigs rosemary, bruised	Pinch of cayenne pepper
4 sprigs thyme, bruised	TO SERVE
1 tbsp dried oregano	Crisp French bread
4 garlic cloves, halved	Natural yogurt

Preheat the oven to 425°F. Wash and dry the mackerel, removing the head and tails, if wished. Season the insides.

Arrange half the lemon slices, half the herbs and half the garlic cloves in the bottom of a large roasting pan. Lay the mackerel on top in a single layer, and cover with the remaining lemon slices, herbs and garlic.

Blend the oil and spices together, pour over the fish, and transfer to the oven for 20 minutes until cooked through.

Serve the mackerel with the pan juices, a spoonful of yogurt, and crisp French bread.

Top: BAKED MACKEREL WITH LEMONS AND SPICES
Bottom: SMOKED HADDOCK PILAF

SWEET POTATO AND SALMON FISH CAKES

Serves 6

The sweet potatoes add an exotic flavor
to this dish.

1 pound salmon fillet, skinned	4 tbsp vegetable oil
1 pound sweet potatoes, cubed	**TOMATO SAUCE**
1 tbsp butter	1 tbsp olive oil
8 scallions, chopped	4 shallots, finely chopped
1 garlic clove, crushed	2 tsp chopped fresh thyme
1 fresh green chili, seeded and chopped	1 pound ripe tomatoes, peeled, seeded and diced
2 tbsp chopped fresh cilantro	6 tbsp water
1 tsp ground cumin	2 tsp red wine vinegar
2 eggs, lightly beaten	Pinch of sugar
4 tbsp seasoned flour	Salt and pepper
2 cups fresh white bread crumbs	

Poach the salmon in cold water (see page 94). Cook the sweet potatoes in boiling water for 10-12 minutes until tender, drain well, and mash with a fork. Set aside to cool.

Meanwhile, melt the butter in a skillet, and fry the scallions, garlic and chili for 5 minutes. Stir into the mashed potato with the cilantro, cumin, and seasoning.

Remove the fish from its liquid, and pat dry. Flake the flesh and beat into the potato mixture with half the beaten egg until combined. Cover and chill for 1 hour.

Make the sauce: heat the olive oil in a pan, and fry the shallots for 5 minutes, stir in all the remaining ingredients, and simmer gently for a further 15 minutes. Purée in a blender until smooth, return to the pan, and keep warm.

Shape the fish mixture into 12 rounds, and flatten each one. Dust with a little seasoned flour, and dip firstly in the remaining beaten egg and then in the bread crumbs.

Heat the vegetable oil in a frying pan, and shallow-fry the fish cakes for 3-4 minutes on each side until crisp and golden. Drain on paper towels, and serve with the sauce.

SMOKED HADDOCK HASH

Serves 2

A variation of the classic corned beef hash, this one is made with fish.and is truly scrumptious.

1 pound potatoes, cubed	8 ounces smoked haddock fillet, skinned and cubed
2 tbsp butter	½ cup grated Cheddar cheese
1 red onion, chopped	1 tbsp natural yogurt
1 tsp chopped fresh rosemary	1 tbsp wholegrain mustard
1 tsp chopped fresh thyme	dash of Tabasco sauce

Boil the potatoes for 10-12 minutes until cooked, drain well, and mash roughly.

Melt the butter in a non-stick skillet, and fry the onion and herbs for 5 minutes. Add the haddock, and fry for a further 2-3 minutes until the fish is opaque.

Add the mashed potato with all the remaining ingredients, and stir until evenly combined. Spread the mixture flat to the sides of the pan, and cook over a medium heat for 6-8 minutes until any liquid has evaporated, and the underside of the hash is browned.

Remove from the heat, and loosen the sides and bottom with a spatula. Place an up-turned plate over the skillet, flip over to invert the hash, and serve at once.

Top: SMOKED HADDOCK HASH
Bottom: SWEET POTATO AND SALMON FISH CAKES

SOLE FILLETS WITH HERB SAUCE

Serves 4

A very light summer dish. To make the thyme-scented oil, simply bruise 4 sprigs of thyme, cover with 2 cups extra virgin olive oil and leave to infuse for several days. Alternatively, simply use a good-quality extra virgin olive oil.

≈

3 small sole, skinned and filleted	*4 tbsp dry white wine*
1 tbsp thyme-scented oil (see recipe introduction)	*1¼ cups Fish Stock (see pages 6-7)*
1 cup mixed fresh herbs (basil, chervil, chives, dillweed, parsley)	*1 cup mixed salad greens*

≈

Cut each fillet in half lengthways, season, and brush with the thyme oil. Roll up each fillet and secure with tooth-picks.

Place the herbs in a wide pan, add the wine and stock, and arrange the plaice rolls on top. Bring to a boil, cover and steam for 8-10 minutes until the fish is cooked through. Transfer the fish to a plate, and keep warm.

Purée the herbs and pan juices until very smooth. Pour into a clean pan, bring to a boil, and simmer until reduced by half.

Toss the salad greens with a little more scented oil, and place in the center of 4 warmed plates. Arrange 3 plaice rolls on each plate, pour over the sauce and serve at once.

PASTA WITH SMOKED SALMON

Serves 4

The age-old classic combination of smoked salmon and sour cream is a fabulous addition to fresh pasta.

≈

2 tbsp unsalted butter	*12 ounces smoked salmon, cut into thin strips*
4 shallots, chopped	
Grated rind of 1 lemon	*4 tbsp chopped fresh chervil*
2 tbsp drained capers, washed and chopped	*4 tbsp sour cream*
	¼ tsp freshly grated nutmeg
1 pound fresh fettucine or tagliatelle	*Salmon (red) caviar, to garnish (optional)*

≈

Heat the butter in a large skillet, and fry the shallots, lemon rind and capers for 3 minutes. Remove from the heat. Meanwhile, bring a large pan of water to a boil, and add the salt. Plunge the pasta into the boiling water, return to a boil, and simmer fast for 2 minutes until the pasta is al dente. Strain, reserving 4 tablespoons of the cooking liquid.

Return the skillet to the heat, and stir in the pasta, reserved cooking liquid, smoked salmon, chervil, sour cream and nutmeg.

Reheat for 2 minutes, and serve at once, garnished with the salmon caviar, if wished.

Top Right: SOLE FILLETS WITH HERB SAUCE
Bottom Left: PASTA WITH SMOKED SALMON

RED MULLET NICOISE EN PAPILLOTE

Serves 6

This is my version of a classic recipe for red mullet served with a Niçoise sauce. Here the fish are baked in parchment paper to keep them moist and tender. Ask your fishvendor to prepare the red mullet.

2 tbsp olive oil	2 tbsp capers, drained and
1 red onion, finely chopped	chopped
1 garlic clove, crushed	¼ cup pitted black olives,
4 cups peeled, seeded and diced	halved
ripe tomatoes	Salt and pepper
2 tsp chopped fresh thyme	2 tbsp melted butter
1 tsp dried oregano	3 x 12-ounce red mullet,
2 tbsp red wine	scaled, cleaned and filleted (see
4 anchovy fillets in oil, drained	recipe introduction)
and chopped	

Heat the oil in a saucepan, and fry the onion and garlic for 5 minutes until browned. Add the tomatoes, thyme, oregano and red wine. Bring to a boil, and simmer for 30 minutes.

Stir in the anchovies, capers and olives. Remove from the heat, season to taste, then set aside to cool.

Preheat the oven to 375°F. Cut out 6 large heart shapes from baking parchment, and make a fold down the center of each one.

Brush one half of each heart with a little melted butter. Spoon over a little of the sauce and place a fillet of mullet on top. Fold the other half of paper over to enclose the filling, turning the edges under to seal the package.

Brush each package with the remaining butter, and transfer to a large baking sheet. Bake for 15 minutes, open 1 package to test if the fish is cooked, and serve straight from the packages.

COD FILLETS WITH SPICED CRUST

Serves 4

Wrapping the cod fillets with spinach leaves keeps the fish tender and moist, while the spicy crust becomes crisp and golden.

4 x 5-ounce cod fillets	½ tsp cumin seeds
4 ripe tomatoes, sliced	¼ tsp ground cinnamon
8 large spinach leaves, washed	1 cup fresh bread crumbs
4 sun-dried tomatoes in oil,	¼ cup hazelnuts, toasted and
drained and finely chopped	ground
1 garlic clove, crushed	1 tbsp chopped fresh parsley
Grated zest and juice of	1 egg, separated
½ lemon	1 tbsp water
1 tsp ground coriander	Salt and pepper

Preheat the oven to 400°F. Wash the cod fillets and pat dry. Season well, and top each with tomato slices.

Blanch the spinach leaves in boiling water for 10 seconds until just wilted. Drain, refresh under cold water, and pat dry. Wrap 2 leaves around each cod fillet.

Prepare the crust: in a bowl mix together the sun-dried tomatoes, garlic, lemon zest and juice, spices, bread crumbs, nuts and parsley. Work in the egg yolk and water to form a soft paste.

Lightly beat the egg white, and brush the top of each spinach package. Divide the crust mixture into four. Spread a quarter of the mixture over each package, pressing down firmly, to form a thin layer over the top of each one. Brush with a little more egg white and transfer to a baking dish. Bake for 20-25 minutes, until a skewer inserted in the fish comes out hot.

Brown the crust under a hot broiler, if wished, and serve at once, with a selection of steamed vegetables.

Top: COD FIL   TS WITH SPICED CRUST
Bottom: RED MU1   T NICOISE EN PAPILLOTE

MONKFISH WITH BROCCOLI IN BLACK BEAN SAUCE

Serves 4

Monkfish is particularly good for this dish, as its firm flesh does not fall apart during the cooking process.

~

1 pound skinned monkfish fillet	8 ounces broccoli florets
1 tbsp dark soy sauce	½ cup vegetable stock or Fish Stock (see pages 6-7)
1 tbsp lime juice	2 tbsp black bean sauce
2 tbsp sweet sherry	1 tsp clear honey
1 garlic clove, crushed	1 tsp cornstarch
1 tsp grated fresh ginger root	1 tbsp sunflower oil
1 small fresh red chili, seeded and sliced	1 tsp sesame oil

~

Cut the monkfish into thin slices, and place in a shallow dish. Mix together the soy sauce, lime juice, sherry, garlic, ginger root and chili. Pour over the fish, cover and marinate for 2-4 hours.

Trim the broccoli, cutting the florets in half if large. Blanch in boiling salted water for 1 minute, drain, refresh under cold water, and pat dry.

Pour the marinade juices into a bowl, and stir in the stock, black bean sauce, honey and cornstarch.

Heat the 2 oils in a non-stick wok or large skillet until it starts to smoke. Pat dry the monkfish, and stir-fry for 2 minutes until lightly browned. Add the broccoli, and stir-fry for 2 minutes. Stir in the black bean sauce mixture, and simmer for 3-4 minutes until the broccoli and fish are cooked through. Serve immediately with egg noodles or fragrant Thai rice.

STEAMED MUSSELS WITH GINGER AND CILANTRO

Serves 4

A fragrant broth, infused with ginger root and cilantro, sets off the rich flavor of the mussels in this quick and easy dish.

1¼ cups dry sherry	1 tsp grated fresh ginger root
1¼ cups water	1 garlic clove, crushed
1 small onion, chopped	1 fresh green chili, seeded and chopped
1 small carrot, chopped	1 leek, trimmed and shredded
1 tsp coriander seeds	2 carrots, cut into julienne
2 slices fresh ginger root	Juice of 1 lime
1 garlic clove	Salt and pepper
2 cilantro stalks	**GARNISH**
4½ pounds mussels, scrubbed	2 tbsp chopped fresh cilantro
SAUCE	Grated zest of 1 lime
1 tbsp sunflower oil	
1 tsp sesame oil	

~

To make the stock, place all the ingredients except the mussels in a large pan, bring to a boil, and simmer gently for 30 minutes. Strain the liquid into a clean pan, and boil rapidly until reduced to ⅔ cup.

Prepare the sauce: heat the sunflower and sesame oil together in a large pan, add the ginger root, garlic and chili, and fry for 3 minutes, then add the leek and carrots.

Add the reduced stock, and bring to a boil. Add the mussels, cover and cook for 6-8 minutes until all the mussels are opened, discarding any that remain closed.

Transfer to a large warmed serving dish, sprinkle over the cilantro and lime, and serve immediately.

Top: STEAMED MUSSELS WITH GINGER AND CILANTRO
Bottom: MONKFISH WITH BROCCOLI IN BLACK BEAN SAUCE

BROILED STUFFED SARDINES

Serves 4 - 6

Fresh sardines, one of the most magical of all fish, are served here with a delicious spiced filling.

2 cups trimmed spinach leaves, washed	1 cup fresh bread crumbs
1 garlic clove, crushed	½ cup feta cheese, crumbled
Grated zest of 1 lemon	¼ tsp gound mixed spice
2 tbsp chopped fresh parsley	2 tbsp olive oil
¼ cup pine nuts, toasted and chopped	12 large fresh sardines (about 4 ounces each), scaled and cleaned
2 tbsp raisins	Salt and pepper
8 anchovy fillets canned in oil, drained and chopped	Lemon wedges, to garnish

Place the washed spinach leaves in a pan with no extra water, and heat for 2-3 minutes until just wilted. Drain, squeeze out excess liquid, and chop finely.

Place the spinach in a bowl, and stir in the garlic, lemon zest, parsley, pine nuts, raisins, anchovies, bread crumbs, feta, spice, and half the oil. Set aside for 1 hour for the flavors to infuse.

Preheat the broiler. Wash and dry the sardines, and fill the stomach cavities with the spinach mixture. Brush with the remaining oil and broil for 4-5 minutes on each side until browned and firm to the touch. Serve at once with lemon wedges.

SPANISH-STYLE SHRIMP

Serves 4 - 6

The addition of ground almonds to this classic Spanish dish of fried shrimp, adds a rich nutty flavor.

2 pounds raw jumbo shrimp	Grated zest and juice of
4 tbsp olive oil	1 lemon
4 garlic cloves, chopped	¼ cup ground almonds, toasted
2 small dried red chilies, seeded and chopped	4 tbsp chopped fresh parsley
	Salt and pepper

Wash and dry the shrimp, but leave the head and shells intact.

Heat the oil in a large pan, and fry the garlic, chili and lemon zest for 1 minute until just starting to turn golden. Add the shrimp and stir-fry over a medium heat for 2 minutes, then cover and simmer for 4-5 minutes until cooked through.

Remove the pan from the heat, and stir in the almonds, parsley and lemon juice, season well, and serve.

Top Left: SPANISH-STYLE SHRIMP
Bottom Right: BROILED STUFFED SARDINES

TANDOORI FISH KEBABS

Serves 4

A combination of fish and shrimp is marinated in spicy yogurt and then broiled to make tangy tandoori kebabs.

2 flounder, skinned and filleted	*1 tsp mild curry powder*
16 raw jumbo shrimp	*1 tsp paprika*
1 pound cod fillet, skinned	*¼ tsp chili powder*
2 limes, cut into wedges	*¼ tsp turmeric*
MARINADE	*1 tbsp lemon juice*
1 small onion, very finely	*⅔ cup thick natural yogurt*
chopped	*Salt and pepper*
2 garlic cloves, crushed	*Lime wedges, to garnish*
1 tsp grated fresh ginger root	

Wash and dry the plaice fillets. Cut each one in half lengthways to make 16 thin strips of fish. Roll up, and secure with toothpicks. Peel and de-vein the shrimp, cut the cod fillet into cubes, and place all the fish in a shallow dish.

Combine all the marinade ingredients together, and pour over the seafood. Cover and marinate for 30 minutes. Soak 8 bamboo skewers in cold water for 30 minutes, drain and pat dry.

Preheat the broiler. Thread the fish, shrimp and lime wedges alternately onto the bamboo skewers. Broil for 8–10 minutes, turning and basting, until charred and cooked through.

Place 2 kebabs on each plate, garnish with lime wedges, and serve with a green salad and naan bread.

BROILED SALMON STEAKS

Serves 4

The thick Chinese-style barbecue sauce makes a fragrant golden glaze for the salmon.

2 tbsp hoisin sauce	*1 tsp grated fresh ginger root*
2 tbsp dark soy sauce	*4 x 5-ounce salmon steaks,*
1 tsp sesame oil	*washed and dried*
¼ tsp five-spice powder	**TO SERVE**
2 tsp clear honey	*Garlic bread*
1 garlic clove, crushed	*Mixed salad*

Place all the ingredients except the salmon in a small bowl, and stir well until combined.

Preheat the broiler. Brush each salmon steak with the glaze, and broil for 3–4 minutes on each side, basting with the remaining glaze until golden and cooked through.

Serve at once with garlic bread and a mixed salad.

Top: TANDOORI FISH KEBABS
Bottom: BROILED SALMON STEAKS

SPAGHETTI VONGOLE

Serves 4

A classic pasta dish using the tiny Venus clams. If fresh clams are unavailable, buy the canned ones in their shells. If all else fails, use canned shelled clams in brine.

≈

2 pounds fresh Venus clams
12 ounces dried spaghetti
1 tsp salt
SAUCE
4 tbsp olive oil or oil from sun-dried tomatoes
2 garlic cloves, sliced
1 fresh red chili, seeded and sliced

4 ripe tomatoes, peeled, seeded and diced
½ cup sun-dried tomatoes in oil, drained and sliced
4 tbsp chopped fresh parsley
Freshly grated Parmesan cheese, to serve (optional)

≈

Scrub the clams, and rinse under cold running water for several minutes. Place in a large pan, and steam for 3-4 minutes until the shells have opened, discarding any that remain closed.

Strain off ⅔ cup of liquid, and remove the clams from their shells, if wished.

Bring a large pan of water to a rolling boil, add the salt, and plunge in the spaghetti. Return to a boil, and simmer rapidly for 10 minutes until al dente.

Meanwhile, prepare the sauce: heat the oil in a large wide pan, and fry the garlic and chili for 1 minute. Add the fresh and dried tomatoes, and reserved clam stock. Bring to a boil, simmer for 5 minutes until thickened, then stir in the clams.

Strain the cooked pasta, toss into the sauce with the parsley, stir for 1 minute until heated through. Serve immediately with black pepper and freshly grated Parmesan cheese.

PASTA WITH MUSSELS IN A HERB SAUCE

Serves 4

A truly delicious combination of flavors make this one of my favorite pasta dishes.

≈

4½ pounds large mussels, scrubbed
3 cups dried pasta shapes
1 tsp salt
2 tbsp butter
6 ounces button mushrooms, quartered
HERB SAUCE
6 tbsp virgin olive oil
Grated zest and juice of ½ lemon

1 garlic clove, crushed
4 tbsp chopped mixed fresh herbs (e.g. chives, parsley, basil, thyme)
2 tbsp freshly grated Parmesan cheese
8 anchovy fillets canned in oil, drained and finely chopped
Salt and pepper

≈

Wash the mussels in cold running water, then steam in a large pan for 5 minutes until the shells are opened, discarding any that remain closed.

Strain off and reserve 4 tablespoons of the liquid, and remove the mussels from their shells.

Bring a large pan of water to a rolling boil, add the salt and the pasta, return to a boil, and cook for 10 minutes until al dente.

Meanwhile, make the sauce: whisk together all the ingredients with the reserved mussel stock until blended. Set aside.

Melt the butter in a large wide pan, and fry the mushrooms for 5 minutes until browned. Strain the pasta, and add to the pan with the mussels and herb sauce. Toss for 1 minute until heated through, and serve at once.

Top: PASTA WITH MUSSELS IN A HERB SAUCE
Bottom: SPAGHETTI VONGOLE

PARSNIP NESTS WITH WHITING AND BEETS

Serves 4

Mashed parsnip and potato is piped to make small nests, and filled with a sweet and savory beet and whiting sauce.

1½ pounds parsnips, cubed	*Pinch of sugar*
8 ounces potatoes, peeled and cubed	*Pinch of salt*
	1¼ cups diced cooked beets
4 tbsp walnut oil	*2 tsp balsamic vinegar*
½ cup grated Gruyère cheese	*12 ounces whiting fillets, skinned and cubed*
1 egg yolk	
Salt and pepper	*2 tbsp chopped fresh chives*
FILLING	*Sour cream or natural yogurt, to serve*
2 tbsp walnut oil	
1 onion, sliced	*Chopped fresh chives, to garnish*
1 tsp caraway seeds	

Boil the parsnips and potatoes for 12-15 minutes until cooked. Drain and mash with the oil, cheese, egg yolk, and salt and pepper. Set aside to cool, then transfer to a piping bag fitted with a large star tip.

Meanwhile, make the filling: heat the oil in a heavy-based pan, and fry the onion with the caraway seeds, sugar and salt for 10 minutes. Add the beets and vinegar, cover and cook for a further 10 minutes.

Preheat the oven to 425°F. Oil a large baking sheet, and pipe on four 4-inch circles of the parsnip and potato mash. Then pipe a ring around the edge of each one to form "nests". Bake for 15-20 minutes until golden and crisp.

Return the beet mixture to the heat. Add the whiting and chives, cover and cook for 6-8 minutes.

Remove the potato "nests" from the oven, spoon in the filling, top each one with a spoonful of sour cream or yogurt and serve at once, garnished with chives.

SEAFOOD PIE WITH POTATO CRUST

Serves 6 - 8

A delicious fish pie ideal for mid-week meals, especially as it freezes well.

2 tbsp olive oil	*6 ounces cooked peeled shrimp*
2 leeks, sliced	*¼ tsp grated nutmeg*
3 celery stalks, sliced	**POTATO TOPPING**
⅓ cup all-purpose flour	
⅔ cup dry cider or white wine	*2 pounds potatoes, peeled and cubed*
1¼ cups milk	
½ cup grated sharp cheese	*4 tbsp olive oil*
8-ounce package frozen leaf spinach, thawed	*2 tbsp chopped fresh thyme*
	½ cup freshly grated Parmesan cheese
8 ounces hake or haddock fillet	
8 ounces smoked cod fillet	*Salt and pepper*

Prepare the filling: heat the oil in a large pan, and fry the leeks and celery for 5 minutes. Stir in the flour, and cook for a further minute. Gradually add the cider or wine and then the milk, stirring constantly, until smooth and thickened. Bring to a boil, simmer gently for 5 minutes, then remove from the heat and stir in the cheese.

Drain the spinach, and squeeze out the excess water. Mix with the fish and shrimp, and stir into the cheese sauce. Spoon into a 2-quart pie dish.

Make the topping: preheat the oven to 400°F. Cook the potatoes in boiling salted water for 12-15 minutes until tender, drain well, and mash with the oil, thyme, cheese and seasonings.

Spoon or pipe the mashed potato over the fish, and bake for 50-60 minutes until golden and bubbling. Cover with foil if the topping starts to become over brown.

Top: SEAFOOD PIE WITH POTATO CRUST
Bottom: PARSNIP NESTS WITH WHITING AND BEETS

COD STEAKS WITH CITRUS SAUCE

Serves 4

A wonderfully light and refreshing summer dish served with a selection of vegetables. Use dillweed if fennel fronds are unavailable.

≈≈

4 x 5-ounce cod steaks	*1 pound summer vegetables*
1-2 tbsp olive oil	*(asparagus, corn, carrots, patty*
Juice of 2 oranges	*pans, zucchini, green beans),*
Juice of 1 lemon	*trimmed and sliced as necessary*
4 tbsp dry white wine	*Salt and pepper*
Grated zest of 1 orange	*4 tbsp heavy cream or crème*
Grated zest of ½ lemon	*fraîche, to serve (optional)*
2 tbsp chopped fennel fronds	

≈≈

Preheat the oven to 425°F. Cut 4 large sheets of foil, and brush each with a little oil. Wash and dry the fish, and place 1 steak in the center of each sheet, pulling up the sides to form a bowl.

Mix together the orange juice, lemon juice, wine, citrus zest and fennel, and spoon over the fish. Draw up the edges of foil, and twist together to seal the packages. Place on a large baking sheet, and bake for 15 minutes until cod is cooked.

Meanwhile, steam the vegetables for 3-5 minutes, depending on the size, until tender. Toss with a little oil, and keep warm.

Arrange the vegetables on plates, open up the packages, and arrange the steaks on top of the vegetables. Pour over the juices from the packages, and serve at once, topped with a spoonful of cream or crème fraîche.

TROUT WITH BACON, MUSHROOMS AND SAGE

Serves 4

A classic combination of bacon, mushrooms and sage makes a rich sauce to serve with whole broiled trout.

≈≈

4 x 12-ounce trout, cleaned,	*½ cup port*
heads removed if wished	*½ cup chicken or vegetable*
1½ tbsp olive oil	*stock*
1½ cups chopped bacon	*1 tbsp balsamic vinegar*
8 ounces button mushrooms,	**GARNISH**
wiped	*Lemon wedges*
1 tbsp chopped fresh sage	*Sage leaves*

≈≈

Preheat the broiler. Wash and dry the trout, and season the insides. Brush with a little oil, and broil for 12-15 minutes, turning once, until the skin is browned and the fish feels firm to the touch. Keep warm.

Meanwhile, make the sauce: heat the remaining oil in a pan, and fry the bacon for 3 minutes until browned. Add the mushrooms and sage, and fry for a further 5 minutes until the mushrooms are browned.

Add the port and ignite with a match. Boil rapidly until the flames die down, then pour in the stock and vinegar. Simmer gently for 5 minutes until the sauce is thick and glossy.

Transfer the trout to warmed plates. Spoon over the sauce, and serve immediately, garnished with lemon wedges and sage leaves.

Top: TROUT WITH BACON, MUSHROOMS AND SAGE
Bottom: COD STEAKS WITH CITRUS SAUCE

ITALIAN MIXED SEAFOOD SALAD

Serves 4

This is my version of the classic Italian mixed seafood salad. Use the tiny Venus clams if possible as they are sweet and tender.

≋

12 ounces small raw shrimp, shelled and deveined (see pages 6-7)	1 red bell pepper, seeded and thinly sliced
12 ounces squid, cleaned (see pages 6-7), sliced into rings	2 celery stalks, thinly sliced
1¼ cups Court Bouillon (see pages 6-7)	1 small head fennel, thinly sliced
1 pound fresh mussels	1 cup pitted green olives, halved
1 pound fresh small clams	2 tbsp chopped celery leaves
¾ cup olive oil	1 tbsp chopped fresh basil
3 tbsp lemon juice	Salt and pepper

≋

Wash and dry the shrimp and squid and place in a large pan. Add the court bouillon, bring to a boil, and simmer gently for 4-5 minutes until shrimp and squid are tender. Strain the stock into a clean pan, and reserve the seafood.

Scrub the mussels and clams, and cook in the stock for 5 minutes until the shells have opened. Discard any that remain closed.

Remove the mussels and clams from their shells, and reserve the stock for another recipe.

Place all the seafood in a large bowl, and stir in the oil and lemon juice until well blended. Set aside for 2 hours.

Just before serving, stir in the remaining ingredients, and serve with crusty bread.

SARDINES WITH CAPONATA

Serves 4

A great combination based on Sicilian cooking.

≋

6 tbsp olive oil	2 ripe tomatoes, chopped
1 onion, chopped	1½ tbsp red wine vinegar
1 garlic clove, chopped	1 tsp sugar
2 celery stalks, sliced	12 large sardines
1 tbsp chopped fresh basil	Juice of 1 lemon
1 medium eggplant, diced	2 tbsp pine nuts, toasted
½ cup pitted green olives, halved	Garlic Sauce (see page 32), to serve (optional)
2 tbsp capers	

≋

Heat 2 tablespoons of the oil in a skillet, and fry the onion, garlic, celery and basil for 5 minutes until browned. Transfer the mixture to a bowl with a slotted spoon.

Add the remaining oil to the pan, and fry the eggplant for 5-6 minutes until golden. Add to the onion and celery mixture with the olives and capers.

Place the tomatoes, vinegar and sugar in a saucepan, bring to a boil, cover and simmer gently for 15 minutes. Stir in the vegetable mixture and pine nuts, season to taste, and set aside to cool slightly.

Preheat the broiler. Clean the sardines, and discard the heads and tails, if wished. Brush inside and outside with oil, season, and squeeze over a little lemon juice. Broil the fish for 4-5 minutes on each side, until charred and cooked through.

Spoon the caponata mixture onto individual serving plates, top each with 3 sardines, and serve at once with garlic sauce, if wished.

Top: SARDINES WITH CAPONATA
Bottom: ITALIAN MIXED SEAFOOD SALAD

DINNER
PARTY DISHES

FISH AND SEAFOOD *can make some of the most impressive dinner party dishes; the recipes in this chapter tend to use more exotic fish and some are aimed at those who cook fish and seafood regularly. However not all are difficult to achieve; for example, Monkfish Baked with Bay Leaves and Garlic and Garlic and Whole Sea Bass Baked in Sea Salt are both exotic and yet simple to prepare and suitable for any occasion.*

Many recipes in this chapter do take a little more time, and some, such as the spectacular Elegant Fish Pie, require a lot more skill to insure success, but a little planning ahead goes a long way and I'm sure your guests will agree that the results are well worth that extra effort.

CONTENTS

SQUID INK PASTA WITH SQUID SAUCE

Serves 4

Squid ink is available in packages from good fishvendors, alternatively try to buy squid with their ink sacs still intact.

2 cups all-purpose flour	*6 tbsp olive oil*
1 tsp salt	*2 shallots, chopped*
2 eggs, plus 1 egg yolk	*2 garlic cloves, sliced*
½ tsp squid ink	*4 tbsp chopped fresh parsley*
2 tbsp olive oil	*2 tbsp drained green*
1-2 tbsp water	*peppercorns, lightly crushed*
SQUID SAUCE	*Salt and pepper*
2 pounds baby squid, cleaned	
(see pages 6-7)	

Sift the flour and salt into a large bowl. Make a well in the center, and gradually work in the eggs, egg yolk, squid ink, olive oil, and enough water to form a firm dough. Knead on a lightly floured surface for 5 minutes until elastic, wrap and leave to rest for 30 minutes.

Divide the dough into 8 equal pieces, and using a pasta machine, roll into 8 long thin sheets. Leave to hang over a pole for 5 minutes, then pass through the tagliatelle attachment on the pasta machine. Flour a large clean dish cloth, and curl the tagliatelle into piles. Set aside.

Slice the squid into rings, and the tentacles in half, if large. Wash well and pat dry.

Heat 2 tablespoons of the oil in a large skillet, add the shallots and garlic, and fry for 2 minutes until softened and lightly golden. Add the squid rings and tentacles, and stir-fry over a high heat for 2-3 minutes. Add the parsley and peppercorns to the squid mixture and stir well.

Meanwhile, bring a large pan of water to a boil. Add 2 teaspoons of salt and plunge in the pasta. Return to a boil, and cook for 2-3 minutes until al dente. Drain, and stir into the squid pan with the remaining oil. Stir over a high heat for 1 minute, and serve at once.

BAKED SEA BASS WITH FENNEL AND ARUGULA

Serves 6

The flavors of sea bass and fennel combine to make a wonderful dish. Ask your fishvendor to fillet three small sea bass for you.

6 x 8-ounce sea bass fillets	*6 tbsp dry white wine*
1 onion, sliced	*2 heads fennel*
1 lemon, sliced	*3 tbsp walnut oil*
1 tbsp fennel seeds	*4 cups arugula*
1 tsp white peppercorns	*Freshly grated nutmeg*
4 sprigs thyme	*Salt and pepper*
2 sprigs rosemary	

Preheat the oven to 425°F, and line a roasting pan with foil.

Wash and dry the bass, and pull out any small bones that remain.

Place the onion slices, lemon slices, fennel seeds, peppercorns, herbs and wine in the prepared pan. Arrange the fillets on top, skin-side up.

Cover the pan with a second piece of foil, and bake the fish for about 20 minutes, or until cooked through.

Meanwhile, preheat the broiler. Cut the fennel lengthways into thin slices, brush with a little of the oil, and broil for 6-8 minutes on each side, until golden and tender. Keep warm.

Just before serving, heat the remaining oil in a skillet. Add the arugula, and cook for 1 minute, stirring, until just wilted. Season with nutmeg, and salt and pepper.

Transfer the arugula to warmed plates. Top with the broiled fennel, and arrange a fillet of sea bass on each one. Serve at once, garnished with baked onion slices, fennel seeds and rosemary from the first baking.

Top: SQUID INK PASTA WITH SQUID SAUCE
Bottom: BAKED SEA BASS WITH FENNEL AND ARUGULA

RED SNAPPER CREOLE

Serves 4

This fiery red sauce is typical of Creole cookery, and keeps the fish beautifully moist as it bakes.

4 red snapper (about 12 ounces each), scaled and cleaned	1 tbsp chopped fresh thyme
Salt and pepper	1 pound ripe tomatoes, peeled, seeded and chopped
2 tbsp olive oil	1¼ cups vegetable stock
1 onion, sliced	1-2 tbsp chili sauce
2 red bell peppers, seeded and chopped	1 tsp sugar
2 garlic cloves, crushed	2 tbsp chopped fresh cilantro

Wash and dry the snapper, and season inside and out with salt and pepper. Set aside.

Heat the oil in a large saucepan, and fry the onion, pepper, garlic and thyme for 5 minutes. Add the tomatoes, stock, chili sauce and sugar, bring to a boil, and simmer for 20 minutes.

Preheat the oven to 400°F. Spoon half the sauce into a large casserole, arrange the snapper on top, then spoon over the remaining sauce. Sprinkle with cilantro, cover, and bake for 25 minutes until the snapper are cooked through.

Serve with boiled rice or bread to soak up the juices.

ROASTED FISH WITH GARLIC AND SHALLOTS

Serves 4

Roasting garlic and shallots in their skins allows them to become soft, mellow and totally delicious. Ask your fishvendor to scale and clean the fish.

12 unpeeled garlic cloves	4 tbsp walnut or olive oil
12 unpeeled shallots	Sea salt and pepper
1 dried red chili, seeded and chopped	4 x 12-ounce bream or red mullet, scaled and cleaned (see recipe introduction)
2 tbsp chopped fresh sage	
4 sprigs thyme	

Preheat the oven to 425°F. Place the garlic, shallots, chili, herbs and oil in a large roasting pan, toss well, and sprinkle with sea salt and pepper. Bake for 20 minutes.

Add the fish, making spaces for them to fit in snugly among the vegetables. Return to the oven for 15 minutes, or until the fish are firm to the touch.

Remove the pan from the oven, cover with foil, and leave to rest for 5 minutes. Serve at once.

Top: RED SNAPPER CREOLE
Bottom: ROASTED FISH WITH GARLIC AND SHALLOTS

CHARRED SOLE WITH MEDITERRANEAN VEGETABLES

Serves 4

If possible, cook the sole over a charcoal fire to get the maximum flavor. Otherwise, a broiler will suffice.

2 x 1-pound lemon sole, skinned	*1 eggplant, sliced*
	2 zucchini, sliced
1 red onion, cut into wedges	*4 large flat mushrooms, quartered*
2 red bell peppers, seeded and quartered	**DRESSING**
6 tbsp olive oil	*4 tbsp olive oil*
4 sprigs thyme	*1 tbsp balsamic vinegar*
2 sprigs rosemary	*Pinch of sugar*
2 garlic cloves, chopped	*Salt and pepper*

Wash and dry the sole, and discard the head, tail and fin bones. Cut each one in half widthways to give 4 equal-sized pieces of fish. Cover and set side.

Preheat the oven to 425°F. Place the onion wedges, bell peppers, half the oil, the herbs and garlic in a large roasting pan, and toss well together. Bake for 20 minutes on the top shelf of the oven.

Add the remaining vegetables, stir once, and bake for a further 20 minutes until caramelized.

Blend the dressing ingredients together, and brush a little over the sole. Cook over coals or under a broiler for 6-8 minutes on each side, basting once, until charred and firm to the touch.

Warm the remaining dressing ingredients in a small pan. Arrange the vegetables on individual plates, top with the fish, pour over the dressing, and serve at once.

MONKFISH BAKED WITH BAY LEAVES AND GARLIC

Serves 4

This recipe is based on a dish prepared for me when I was working in Greece. They used an eel, but I prefer to use monkfish. Ask your fishvendor to prepare the monkfish, if wished.

1 x 2-pound monkfish tail, skin and tail removed	*Salt and pepper*
	2 tbsp olive oil
8 bay leaves	*6 tbsp dry white wine*
1 lemon, sliced	*1 onion, sliced*
8 garlic cloves	*6 sprigs rosemary*

Preheat the oven to 425°F. Carefully cut down each side of the monkfish bone, and remove it without cutting the body completely in half.

Place the bay leaves, half the lemon slices and the garlic cloves in the center of the fish. Season well and tie together with string, at 1-inch intervals.

Heat half the oil in a heavy-based, non-stick skillet. Fry the fish for 2-3 minutes, turning, until well browned all over. Add the wine, boil for 1 minute, and remove from the heat.

Place the onion slices, remaining lemon slices and rosemary sprigs in a roasting pan. Sit the browned fish on top and pour over the pan juices. Bake for 30 minutes until a skewer inserted in the center comes out hot.

Place the fish on a serving dish, and remove the string. Cover with foil, and leave to rest for 5 minutes before serving.

Top: MONKFISH BAKED WITH BAY LEAVES AND GARLIC
Bottom: CHARRED SOLE WITH MEDITERRANEAN VEGETABLES

TUNA TERIYAKI WITH GLAZED TOMATOES

Serves 4

The fish is seared over a high heat to brown the outside, leaving the inside raw, making a delicious contrast in textures. Plunging the seared fish into cold water halts the cooking process.

1 x 1-pound tuna loin or steak	½ cup boiling water
3 tbsp tamari soy sauce	2 tbsp olive oil
6 tbsp water	8 ounces red and yellow cherry tomatoes, halved
2 tbsp dry sherry	1 tbsp clear honey
1 tbsp rice or wine vinegar	Salt and pepper
½ cup dried shiitake mushrooms	

Cut the tuna loin or steak into four. Wash, pat dry and place in a shallow dish.

Blend together the soy sauce, water, sherry and rice or wine vinegar and pour over the tuna. Cover and leave to marinate for at least 2 hours.

Soak the dried mushrooms in the boiling water for 30 minutes. Drain well, reserving the liquid, and slice.

Drain the marinade from the tuna, and reserve. Heat half the oil in a heavy-based skillet, until just starting to smoke. Dry the tuna and seal in the hot oil for 1-2 minutes, browning on all sides. Remove from the heat and immediately plunge into cold water. Pat dry.

Sear the tomato halves, cut-side down on the griddle, and set aside.

Heat the remaining oil in a small skillet, add the mushrooms, and fry for 2 minutes. Add the reserved tuna marinade and mushroom liquid, bring to a boil, then cover and simmer for 10 minutes. Stir in the honey, add the tomatoes, and simmer for 1 minute.

Cut the tuna strips into very thin slices, and serve with the caramelized tomato sauce.

BAKED TROUT WITH THAI SPICES

Serves 4

The curry paste requires cilantro roots for a truly authentic flavor. Bunches of fresh cilantro usually come with the roots still attached, which need washing well. Alternatively, use two cilantro stalks.

4 medium trout, cleaned	4 garlic cloves, chopped
RED CURRY PASTE	2 shallots, chopped
	1 tsp ground black pepper
8 dried red chilies, seeded and chopped	**SAUCE**
8 cilantro roots, washed and chopped	1 bunch scallions, sliced
	4 tbsp dark soy sauce
1 tbsp grated fresh ginger root	4 tbsp dry sherry
2 stalks lemon grass, chopped	4 tbsp water
4 kaffir lime leaves, shredded, or grated zest of 2 limes	Juice of 2 limes
	2 tbsp chopped fresh cilantro

Preheat the oven to 400°F. Wash and dry the trout, cut 4 slashes in each side.

Make the curry paste: place all the ingredients in a blender, and purée until smooth. Spread the mixture all over the inside and outside of the trout.

Lightly oil 4 sheets of foil, and place a trout in the center of each one. Draw up the edges of the foil, leaving a gap in the top.

Combine all the sauce ingredients together, and divide between the packages, spooning the sauce through the gaps. Seal the edges by twisting the foil over.

Place the packages on a large baking sheet. Transfer to the oven, and bake for 20-25 minutes until the trout are cooked through. Serve at once.

Top: BAKED TROUT WITH THAI SPICES
Bottom: TUNA TERIYAKI WITH GLAZED TOMATOES

HALIBUT WITH VERMICELLI

Serves 6

Based on a classic Spanish recipe, this delicious dish using dried vermicelli pasta needs to be eaten as soon as it is cooked, to prevent it from becoming dry.

6 x 5-ounce halibut steaks	*4 ripe tomatoes, peeled, seeded*
1 quart Fish Stock (see	*and diced*
pages 6-7)	*Pinch of saffron strands*
2 cups tomato juice	*1 tsp ground cumin*
2 tbsp olive oil	*Pinch cayenne pepper*
4 garlic cloves, crushed	*8 ounces vermicelli, broken into*
	short lengths

Start by poaching the fish: wash and dry the halibut steaks, and place in a large pan to fit in a single layer. Add the fish stock and tomato juice, bring to a boil, simmer for 1 minute, and remove from the heat.

Strain 1 quart of the tomato-flavored stock carefully into a jug, and allow the fish to cool in the remaining stock.

Heat the oil in a large pan, and fry the garlic for 2 minutes. Add the tomatoes, and fry for 10 minutes. Stir in the saffron, spices and vermicelli, and fry for 1 minute.

Add the fish stock, bring to a boil, and simmer for 10 minutes until the vermicelli is cooked.

When the vermicelli is almost ready, gently reheat the fish in its stock. Transfer the fish to serving plates, and serve the vermicelli separately.

BROILED LOBSTER WITH FENNEL SAUCE

Serves 2

Rich and delicious, the perfect dish for a celebration. As the lobster is to be cooked twice, ask your fishvendor to undercook the lobster for you; otherwise after broiling, the meat may become tough.

2 cooked lobsters (about	**FENNEL SAUCE**
1 pound each) (see recipe	*⅔ cup olive oil*
introduction)	*¼ cup boiling water*
MARINADE	*Juice of 1 lemon*
6 tbsp olive oil	*1 garlic clove, crushed*
2 garlic cloves, crushed	*2 tbsp chopped fennel fronds*
1 tbsp chopped fennel fronds	*1 tbsp chopped fresh parsley*
1 tsp dried oregano	

Cut the lobsters in half through the center of their heads and bodies. Arrange cut-side up in a shallow dish. Combine the marinade ingredients in a bowl, and pour over the lobsters. Cover, and leave to marinate for 1 hour.

Make the sauce: place the oil in a bowl, gradually whisk in the boiling water, and then all the remaining ingredients. Continue to whisk for 1 minute until the sauce is slightly thickened.

Preheat the broiler. Baste the lobsters with a little of the fennel sauce and broil for 5-6 minutes until sizzling and golden, basting frequently.

Serve hot with the remaining sauce.

Top: HALIBUT WITH VERMICELLI
Bottom: BROILED LOBSTER WITH FENNEL SAUCE

ELEGANT FISH PIE

Serves 8

An attractive fish-shaped puff pastry pie makes a
stunning dinner party dish. If using samphire,
soak in plenty of cold water for 1 hour to
remove excess saltiness.

≈≈

2 tbsp butter
1 onion, finely chopped
⅓ cup all-purpose flour
1¼ cups sour cream
¼ tsp ground mace
Salt and pepper
12 ounces sole fillets, skinned

*12 ounces salmon fillets,
skinned*
Grated zest and juice of 1 lime
*6 ounces samphire, soaked and
drained, or asparagus tips*
*1 pound puff pastry, thawed if
frozen*
Beaten egg, to glaze

Melt the butter in a pan and fry the onion for 5 minutes,
stir in the flour and cook for 1 minute. Gradually add the
cream, stirring until smooth. Cook for 2 minutes, then
remove from the heat, and add the mace and seasonings.
Cover the surface with baking parchment, and leave to
cool.

Wash and dry the fish fillets, and pull out any remaining
bones. Cut the flesh into large cubes. Stir the fish into the
cooled cream sauce with the lime zest and juice. Cover
and set aside.

Preheat the oven to 425°F, and lightly oil a large
baking sheet. Blanch the samphire or asparagus tips in
boiling salted water for 2 minutes. Drain, refresh under
cold water, and pat dry.

Roll out half the pastry dough to a rectangle about 10 x
12 inches, and cut out a large fish shape. Transfer to the
prepared baking sheet. Roll out the remaining pastry to a
slightly larger rectangle.

Carefully arrange the samphire or asparagus and the fish
mixture over the pastry fish, leaving a 1-inch border
around the edges. Dampen the edges, and place the rectangle of pastry over the top, pressing the edges together
well to seal. Trim the top layer to match the base, press
the edges together and flute.

Mark scale and fin shapes over the pastry with a small
knife, and brush with the beaten egg. Bake for 20
minutes, then lower the oven temperature to 375°F, and
bake for a further 10-15 minutes until the pastry is risen,
golden, and a skewer inserted in the center comes out hot.

SMOKED SALMON AND POTATO TORTE

Serves 8-10

Layers of thinly sliced potato and smoked salmon are baked in a cake pan to make a really fabulous pie.

≈

2 tbsp olive oil	1 cup ricotta or low-fat
1½ pounds potatoes	curd cheese
Pepper	1 garlic clove, crushed
12 ounces smoked salmon	1 tbsp chopped fresh dillweed
	6 ripe tomatoes, thinly sliced

≈

Preheat the oven to 425°F, and lightly oil a 9-inch springform pan.

Cut the potatoes into wafer-thin slices, using a sharp knife or food processor fitted with the slicing blade.

Arrange a single layer of potato slices over the base of the prepared pan, season with pepper, and top with a layer of smoked salmon.

Beat the cheese, garlic and dillweed together. Carefully spread one-third of the mixture over the smoked salmon. Arrange a layer of tomato slices over the cheese. Repeat all the layers, finishing with a final layer of potato.

Pour over the remaining oil, and bake for about 1 hour until the potatoes are golden, and a skewer inserted in the center comes out hot. Cover the torte with foil if it starts to burn.

Remove from the oven, and allow to cool in the pan for 5 minutes. Unmold the torte, and using a very sharp knife, cut into wedges to serve.

SALMON FILO PACKAGES WITH ARUGULA PESTO

Serves 4

The peppery arugula mellows as it cooks inside the filo packages, giving a delicate and delicious sauce for the salmon.

≈

4 x 4-ounce salmon fillets, skinned	2 juniper berries, crushed
8 small sheets of filo pastry, thawed if frozen	Grated zest and juice of ½ lemon
4 tbsp olive oil	1 garlic clove, crushed
ARUGULA PESTO	¼ cup pine nuts, toasted
2 cups arugula leaves	¼ cup low-fat cream cheese
	Salt and pepper

≈

Preheat the oven to 425°F, and lightly oil a baking sheet.

Start by making the pesto: place all the ingredients in a blender and purée to form a fairly smooth paste. Adjust the seasoning, cover and set aside.

Wash and pat dry the salmon fillets, and pull out any remaining bones.

Brush each sheet of filo pastry with oil. Place 2 sheets together and sit a salmon fillet in the center. Spread a quarter of the pesto over each salmon fillet. Carefully fold over the pastry to enclose the filling and seal the package. Brush with oil, and transfer to the baking sheet. Repeat to make 4 packages.

Bake for 20-25 minutes until the pastry is crisp and golden. Serve with asparagus or a salad.

Top: SMOKED SALMON AND POTATO TORTE
Bottom: SALMON FILO PACKAGES WITH ARUGULA PESTO

WHOLE SEA BASS BAKED IN SEA SALT

Serves 4

The sight of this magnificent fish in a golden crust of sea salt is sure to bring gasps of appreciation from your dinner guests. The fish cooks slowly in its blanket of salt, which comes away easily once cooked, leaving a succulent and quite delicious fish underneath.

1 x 4-pound sea bass, scaled and cleaned	2 whole garlic cloves
2 sprigs thyme	Salt and pepper
2 sprigs parsley	1 pound sea salt
½ lemon, sliced	4 egg whites
	Lemon wedges, to serve

Preheat the oven to 375°F. Wash and dry the bass. Stuff the stomach cavity with the herbs, lemon slices, garlic and seasonings.

Place the sea salt in a bowl. Lightly whisk the egg whites until frothy, then stir into the salt until mixed.

Oil a large, narrow baking dish and place the fish into it. Spread over the sea salt mixture to completely coat the bass. Transfer to the oven, and bake for 40 minutes until the salt is golden.

Remove from the oven, and leave to rest for 10 minutes. Break open the salt covering, and serve the fish with lemon wedges.

DOVER SOLE WITH FRESH HERB SAUCE

Serves 2

Dover sole has such a superlative flavor that simple broiling is my favorite cooking method; a fresh-tasting herb sauce, the perfect accompaniment.

2 Dover sole, cleaned and skinned	⅔ cup Fish Stock (see pages 6-7)
Olive oil, for brushing	4 tbsp chopped fresh herbs
2 tbsp butter	2 tbsp drained capers
2 shallots	Grated rind of 1 lemon
⅔ cup dry white wine	¼ cup unsalted butter

Wash and dry the fish, and brush liberally with olive oil. Preheat the broiler.

Meanwhile, melt the butter in a small pan, and fry the shallots for 3 minutes until softened but not browned. Add the wine and stock, and boil rapidly until the sauce is reduced by half.

Place the fish under the broiler, and cook for 6-8 minutes on each side until firm to the touch.

While the fish is cooking, add the herbs, capers and lemon rind to the wine sauce. Simmer, covered, for 5 minutes. Whisk in the butter, a little at a time, until the sauce is glossy. Keep warm.

Arrange the sole on serving plates, and pour over the herb sauce. Serve at once, garnished with fresh herbs, and accompanied by steamed vegetables and sautéed potatoes.

Top: WHOLE SEA BASS BAKED IN SALT
Bottom: DOVER SOLE WITH FRESH HERB SAUCE

SHRIMP AND FENNEL RISOTTO

Serves 6

A delicious creamy risotto,
ideal for a winter evening.

1½ pound small raw shrimp	⅔ cup white wine
1½ quarts water	2 ripe tomatoes, peeled, seeded
Pinch of saffron strands	and diced
3 tbsp olive oil	2 tbsp chopped fresh dillweed
1 onion, chopped	½ cup soft goat cheese
2 garlic cloves, crushed	Salt and pepper
1 head fennel, trimmed and	Freshly grated Parmesan
diced	cheese, to serve (optional)
1¾ cups arborio rice	

Peel and devein the shrimp (see pages 6-7). Place the heads and shells in a pan with the cold water and a pinch of salt. Bring to a boil, skim the surface, and simmer gently for 20 minutes.

Pour the liquid through a fine strainer into a clean pan. Boil rapidly until reduced to about 1 quart. Add the saffron strands, and set aside to infuse.

Heat the oil in a large heavy-based pan, and fry the onion, garlic and fennel for 5 minutes. Add the rice, and stir-fry for 2 minutes.

Add the wine, and boil rapidly until almost evaporated. Add about ⅔ cup of the saffron stock, and simmer until absorbed. Continue adding the stock, a little at a time, and stirring frequently, until almost all the liquid is used up (about 25 minutes).

Stir the shrimp into the pan with the remaining stock, and cook for 6-8 minutes, until the shrimp are pink.

Stir in the remaining ingredients and heat through. Season to taste, and serve at once with some freshly grated Parmesan, if wished.

SWORDFISH KEBABS WITH PUY LENTILS

Serves 4

If you cannot find Puy lentils, use
brown lentils instead.

⅔ cup Puy lentils	2 tbsp chopped fresh basil
7 tbsp olive oil	½ cup pitted black olives,
1 red onion, diced	chopped
1 small red bell pepper, seeded	1½ pounds fresh swordfish
and diced	steak, cubed
1 garlic clove, crushed	Salt and pepper
Juice of 1 lemon	

Soak the lentils in cold water for 4 hours.

Drain the lentils well, place in a pan, and cover with cold water. Bring to a boil, simmer gently for 35-40 minutes until tender, then drain.

Heat 2 tablespoons of the oil in a skillet, and fry the onion, pepper and garlic for 5 minutes. Add the lemon juice, lentils, basil and olives, and simmer gently for 3 minutes. Keep warm.

Preheat the broiler. Thread the cubed swordfish onto 8 small skewers. Brush with a little of the remaining oil, and place under the broiler. Cook for 4-5 minutes, turning and basting, until golden and firm to the touch.

Stir the remaining oil into the lentil mixture, and heat through. Spoon onto warmed plates and top with the kebabs. Serve at once with a crisp green salad.

Top Right: SWORDFISH KEBABS WITH PUY LENTILS
Bottom Left: SHRIMP AND FENNEL RISOTTO

FLOUNDER WITH WILD MUSHROOM SAUCE

Serves 4

Dried porcini mushrooms add a wonderful depth of flavor to this dish. They are expensive, but you only need a small amount.

2 tbsp dried porcini mushrooms	8 ounces mixed wild mushrooms, (e.g. chanterelles, porcini, blewits, oyster)
⅔ cup boiling water	
¼ cup brandy	2 flounder, filleted
⅔ cup vegetable stock	¼ cup unsalted butter, softened
4 tbsp olive oil	1 tbsp chopped fresh parsley
2 shallots, chopped	Salt and pepper

Soak the dried porcini mushrooms in the boiling water for 30 minutes. Strain, reserving the liquid, and chop the porcini mushrooms.

Place the reserved mushroom stock, brandy, and vegetable stock in a pan. Bring to a boil, and simmer to reduce until only about ⅔ cup remains.

Heat half the oil in a skillet, and fry the shallots for 3 minutes. Add the soaked and fresh mushrooms, and stir-fry for 5 minutes. Cover and keep warm.

Heat the broiler, brush the fish fillets with the remaining oil, and broil for 5-6 minutes until cooked.

Meanwhile, bring the reduced stock to a rolling boil. Whisk in the butter, a little at a time, until the sauce is thickened and glossy.

Transfer the fish to warmed plates, spoon over the mushrooms, and pour over the sauce. Sprinkle with parsley and serve at once.

FILLET OF TURBOT WITH BRAISED LEEKS

Serves 4

Turbot is an expensive fish and may be difficult to find, but its delicate flavor works well with the leeks. Flounder makes a good substitute.

1 pound baby leeks, trimmed	2 tbsp chopped fresh chervil
2 tbsp butter	Salt and pepper
2 shallots, quartered	4 small turbot fillets
2 tsp yellow mustard seeds	1 tbsp olive oil
4 tbsp dry sherry	

Cut the leeks into thin slices. Melt the butter in a pan, add the shallots and mustard seeds, and fry for 3 minutes. Add the leeks, and fry for a further 3 minutes.

Add the sherry, cover and braise over a low heat for 5-8 minutes until the leeks are tender. Stir in the chervil, and season to taste.

Meanwhile, preheat the broiler. Wash the turbot fillets, and pat dry. Brush with a little oil, and place under the broiler for 6-8 minutes until cooked through.

Serve the turbot on a bed of braised leeks, with baby potatoes and carrots.

Top: FLOUNDER WITH WILD MUSHROOM SAUCE
Bottom: FILLET OF TURBOT WITH BRAISED LEEKS

MONKFISH WITH PEARS

Serves 4

The pears combine surprisingly well with the monkfish to make an unusual, but satisfying dish.

4 tbsp walnut oil	⅔ cup dry cider or unsweetened
1 red onion, sliced	apple juice
1 garlic clove, crushed	⅔ cup vegetable stock
2 tsp chopped fresh sage	1 tbsp wholegrain mustard
1 tsp fennel seeds	2 tbsp unsalted butter
2 x 1-pound monkfish tails,	2 ripe pears, cored and
filleted in half	thickly sliced
1 tbsp Calvados or brandy	

Preheat the oven to 400°F. Heat the oil in a skillet, and fry the onions, garlic, sage and fennel seeds for 5 minutes, until golden. Using a slotted spoon, transfer to a roasting pan.

Increase the heat under the skillet, add the monkfish, and fry for 3-4 minutes until well browned all over. Place in the roasting pan on top of the onion mixture.

Pour the Calvados or brandy into the skillet, ignite and flame. When the flame dies down, add the cider or apple juice, stock and mustard. Bring to a boil, and add to the roasting pan. Transfer to the oven, and bake for 15 minutes.

After 10 minutes, melt the butter in a clean skillet, and fry the pears for 3-4 minutes until browned on both sides. Remove from the skillet, and keep warm.

Remove the roasting pan from the oven. Strain the juices into the skillet. Cover the monkfish with foil, and keep warm.

Bring the cooking juices to a boil, and simmer to reduce and thicken slightly. Arrange the onion mixture and pears on a serving dish, top with the monkfish fillets, and pour over the sauce. Serve at once with steamed vegetables and baby new potatoes.

SALMON WITH POTATO AND ARTICHOKE SALAD

Serves 4

The warm potato salad in a luscious artichoke cream complements the salmon perfectly - a lovely simple summer dish.

4 x 5-ounce salmon fillets,	14-ounce can artichoke hearts,
skinned	drained
2½ cups Court Bouillon (see	Juice of ½ lemon
pages 6-7)	2 tbsp chopped fresh dillweed
POTATO SALAD	½ small garlic clove, crushed
1 pound baby potatoes, halved	4 tbsp mayonnaise
	Salt and pepper

Wash the fish fillets, and pat dry. Cut each fillet into 3 thick slices or large escalopes and place in a pan. Add the court bouillon, bring to a boil, then remove from the heat and leave for 10 minutes.

Transfer the fish to a plate and allow to cool.

Make the salad: simmer the potatoes in boiling water for 10-12 minutes until cooked. Drain well, and place in a serving bowl.

Place all the remaining ingredients in a blender, and purée to form a fairly smooth sauce. Mix with the potatoes. Serve the salmon and salad at room temperature.

Top: SALMON WITH POTATO AND ARTICHOKE SALAD
Bottom: MONKFISH WITH PEARS